My Lucky Pants

The Impact of Cognitive Biases in Sport

Robert Prior-Wandesforde

ISBN: 978-1-9162308-5-9

To the sport obsessed

CONTENTS

ACKNOWLEDGMENTS

With huge thanks to those that have read the various drafts, including my wife, Angela, and editor, Jerry. I am also very grateful to my son, Ben, for his help with the production of the book cover.

Finally, a big thank you to all the researchers and authors of the various academic and other studies I have referred to in this book.

PREFACE

My love affair with sport began at a tender age. One of my earliest memories is playing table tennis when I was barely taller than the table, while I also remember obsessively watching snooker on a black and white TV. The English summer saw me square-eyed as well, my attention focussed on a hard, red ball and thirteen men wearing white. Test cricket was my passion and remains so. When I wasn't in front of the goggle box, I was often in the garden playing cricket with my elder brother — I can still smell the freshly cut grass — or kicking a ball around with friends, generally till dark.

Living in Sussex until the age of 16, I was a big supporter of Brighton and Hove Albion, attending the old Goldstone Ground as a regular birthday treat. Peter Ward was my hero, a quick Google search revealing that he joined the club for a whopping £4,000 in 1975! Sussex was my cricket team and Paul Parker — one of the many English one-cap wonders — my favourite player. To further illustrate my vintage, Imran Khan, the brilliant all-rounder and Pakistan Prime Minister to be, was the team's biggest star at the time.

Sadly, I wasn't altogether successful when it came to

playing competitive sport, my zenith being to represent Sussex County Colts as a batter and occasional off-spinner in a couple of matches during the late-1970s. Having been run out for a duck on debut, it wasn't long before I suffered a season-ending appendicitis!

Life then took me into higher education and various economist roles, including in Asia, before I retired early to study psychology and to write. As an author my particular interest has been the powerful role played by comparisons in shaping our mental health and the decisions we take. I am also fascinated by the strange things we think and do as we go about our everyday lives, and I wrote a book exploring the psychological factors behind them — from the reasons for our love-hate relationship with social media to why everybody believes that they are a better-than-average driver!

Given my sporting obsessions, it was a natural progression to observe, explore and write about the many oddities that occur on and off the field of play. Researching the subject has proved every bit as rich, intriguing and entertaining as I thought it would be. My hope now is that you agree.

INTRODUCTION

"It's weird not to be weird"

John Lennon

The playing and watching of sport are rife with psychological peculiarities. Consider the following:

Otherwise sane, sensible people become convinced that certain rituals, including the wearing of 'lucky pants,' will influence results; some players perform superbly in one competition and appallingly in another of equal standard; two individuals can watch the same event and come to polar opposite views about a participant; managers are sacked at the drop of a hat by owners who made their fortune investing for the long term; players are bought because they did well in competitions widely known to be unrepresentative; substitutes magically become a lot better when their teammates are performing badly; and most players find defending a trophy or leading a race far harder than winning it in the first place or coming from behind.

In each case, our thoughts and deeds, at least from an outsider's perspective, appear rather weird, often self-defeating. The extent to which this matters depends on the nature of our involvement with sport. For many of us, such oddities are simply entertaining quirks, subjects for a water cooler chat. For others, they are a source of irritation or the starting point of a discussion/argument. For some, however, they can have serious emotional and financial consequences. Think about the money lost by over-paying for a player, the turmoil created by a series of unwise bets on sporting outcomes or the impact of poor decision-making on players' careers.

So, what is that makes us — and I mean *all* of us — think in bizarre ways and do so repeatedly, failing to learn from our mistakes? Cognitive Biases — inbuilt mental processes that systematically lead to irrational conclusions — are often responsible.

Such biases are effectively the unintended consequences of the way the human brain, conditioned by millennia of hunter-gathering activities, has evolved. Our methods of thinking simply haven't had the chance to adjust to the very different challenges posed by modern living, including the playing and watching of organised sport. As a result, we are left using a tool moulded by experiences that we don't often come across. Let's face it, the closest most of us get to hunting and gathering these days is attempting to gain more followers on social media, while the biggest physical danger we normally encounter is crossing the road! With this in mind, it is perhaps surprising just how well our brains *do* perform these days.

Much has been written about the impact of cognitive biases in business and finance. Far less so in sport. And yet sport — jam-packed as it is with decisions, judgements and predictions, often made under significant pressure — is the perfect environment for such biases to operate. If we are to better understand sport, it is essential to better understand why, how and in what circumstances these biases and other thinking peculiarities operate. This is what the book is about. Designed for armchair sports fans, sporting participants, and those interested in the wider implications of cognitive biases, it examines many of the seemingly inexplicable, sometimes amusing events that occur on and off the field.

Being born and bred in England, my focus is the strange goings on in and around the country's national sports of football and cricket. But the findings are relevant to most sports and indeed other aspects of our lives, many of which I explored in my book '*Fallibilities & Peculiarities: Exploring the Odd Things We Think & Do*.'[1]

In the book, I begin by describing our methods of thinking and how these can create oddities, before delving into each of the areas below as they relate to sport. At the end of each chapter, I have provided an "in brief" recap of the most interesting issues contained within.

- Luck and destiny
- Judgements and decisions
- Predictions and pundits
- Form and 'The Zone'
- Referee and umpire bias
- Winning and losing
- Crowds and fandom

1
STRANGE WAYS

"Nothing is so difficult as not deceiving oneself"

Ludwig Wittgenstein, Austrian philosopher

To understand our strange thoughts and actions when it comes to sport, we must first understand a bit more about how we think. Psychologists explain that we have two methods of thinking, typically and rather unoriginally labelled Systems 1 and 2.

System 1 refers to unconscious thoughts. Always operating, it is designed to provide quick, effortless solutions to every situation we face. The solutions stem from our instinct, intuition and beliefs and represent our brain's initial response to the questions posed of it.

System 2 works very differently. It supplies more considered responses that rely on our intelligence, experiences and other problem-solving abilities, making it far slower and more effortful to use. Unlike System 1 it requires frequent periods of rest to work effectively and cannot multitask. To illustrate this last point, try working out the answer to 13 x 46 in your head while *simultaneously* spelling the word 'impossible.' Our brain requires us to tackle these tasks independently, unless you happen to have committed the multiplication answer to memory.

System 1 Thinking	**System 2 Thinking**
Always active	Requires rest
Involves no conscious effort	Involves conscious effort
Driven by instinct, intuition and beliefs	Driven by experience and learning
Quick to give answers	Slow to give answers
Provides instinctive answers	Provides considered answers
Takes shortcuts and makes big assumptions	Takes fewer shortcuts and makes fewer assumptions
Good at multitasking	Bad at multitasking
Provides suggestions to System 2	Can instruct System 1 but often chooses not to
Makes mistakes	Makes mistakes

System 1 thinking is fundamental to our survival. Faced with life-or-death situations, we don't necessarily have the luxury to consider all possibilities, but must act on instinct. If this wasn't the case, we would have undoubtedly joined the dodos by now.

It is vital at a more mundane level as well. Consider what happens when we wake up in the morning: we immediately recognise our partner and everything around us; we know that the cooker is hot once we have turned it on; we remember how to drive the car and our route to work; we recognise that our colleague is in a bad mood from their expression; we immediately understand what somebody says to us — and so on throughout the day. If we didn't do any of this and had to consciously think our way through it all, just imagine how long it would take to get out of the door, let alone achieve anything meaningful.

There are, however, occasions when automatic, speedy answers can prove disadvantageous. Let's consider a few sporting examples:

- Say we are trying to predict the score of a football match. Noting that on the two previous occasions the teams met, the game finished in a 4-3 win for the home side, System 1 will promote the idea that another 4-3 outcome is likely, when in reality it isn't. A very small proportion of games end with such a score line.
- Watching the highlights of a cricket match, we see a batter scoring a century. System 1 will tell us that they would be a great addition to our team and the club should recruit them. What the highlights didn't reveal, however — and System 1 will therefore ignore — was the luck they had in reaching the score, while it will also fail to recognise that the player was batting against a team missing their two key bowlers.
- We are playing in defence against a team with a relatively short striker and have the responsibility of marking the player at set pieces. System 1 will suggest that we needn't worry too much about their aerial ability. As it turns out, however, they are great in the air.

- We are a spectator at a match involving a player we believe is massively overrated. They do well most of the time, but also make a few mistakes. System 1 will ensure that the mistakes gain greater prominence in our mind.

In each of these instances, our instinctive reaction works to *reduce* the probability of success and good judgement. By engaging System 2 and thinking more deeply about the issue, we could avoid making a financially painful or embarrassing mistake. The thing is — and this is the really interesting bit — most of us won't. We stick with our initial, knee-jerk response and (potentially) make the mistake. The story doesn't end here either. Faced with a similar situation in the future, we will probably make the same mistake again, failing to learn from our previous experience. Why? What is that makes us think and behave against our own best interests in certain circumstances?

There are several factors:

First, conscious thought involves effort, which we are naturally reluctant to expend. As Daniel Kahneman put it in his book '*Thinking, Fast and Slow*'[7]:

"*A general law of least effort applies to cognitive as well as physical exertion. The law asserts that if there are several ways of achieving the same goal, people will gravitate to the least demanding course of action. Laziness is built deep into our nature.*"

This seems about right to me! Just as it is much easier to give up when exercising than continue through the pain, it is far simpler to rely on the first thought that comes to mind than to dig around for a better alternative. 'Proper' thinking is uncomfortable too.

Second, conscious thought occupies valuable time:

time that we generally prefer using in other, more pleasurable and less demanding ways.

Third, we are poor at identifying those circumstances where more considered thinking is likely to trump instinctive answers or at least not in sufficient time to act accordingly. If we notice the error of our ways at all, it is usually after the event.

Fourth, we might spend a lot of time and effort thinking through issues and still come up with the same answer and/or the wrong one. System 2 is not guaranteed to provide the right answer either. It is only as good as our underlying intelligence, knowledge and experience permits.

A shortcut to problems

By operating in these ways, we open ourselves up to many cognitive biases and other peculiarities. Problems emanate mainly from the array of shortcuts — termed 'heuristics' by psychologists — used by System 1 to arrive at the quick, effortless answers that it does.

These include predicting the future simply by extrapolating the past; stereotyping others; relying heavily on emotional responses; failing to look beyond what is presented or consider alternative scenarios; generating simple causal narratives for complicated outcomes and genuine coincidences; overestimating the importance of recent events and the frequency of unusual episodes; believing the past is easy to explain; drawing powerful conclusions from simple but misleading comparisons; and providing answers to easier questions than those actually asked of us.

While it is tempting to believe that we ourselves are not susceptible to such issues, we would be wrong to do so. Such is their instinctive nature, *everybody* experiences cognitive biases, and while some are better at avoiding their consequences than others, we all act upon them on occasion. Even Professor Kahneman — who spent a lifetime researching these biases, becoming a Nobel Laureate in the process — admitted that he is just as prone to thinking fallacies as the rest of us.

But even if we can't rid ourselves of these biases completely, there is still plenty we can do. This includes identifying the sort of circumstances that provoke odd thinking, understanding why we think in these ways and examining the consequences of so doing. The book will explore all these things.

In brief

Instinct plays a huge role in determining what we think as we go about our day-to-day activities and deal with an uncertain future. Such mental processes are usually incredibly helpful but can create oddities in certain circumstances. Not just any old oddities either: those that are both foreseeable and yet strangely difficult to avoid.

As human beings, we are, of course, also capable of more in-depth, conscious thought. We are often reluctant to resort to it, however, given the time and effort required to do so. Call it laziness or efficiency, this inherent trait means we are heavily inclined to rely on easy yet often biased or irrational answers rather than search for potentially better ones. This can be the case even when we have plenty of time at our disposal.

It is these factors that explain why we think in peculiar ways and fail to learn from previous mistakes. We are nothing if not curious, not least when it comes to sport.

2
LUCK AND DESTINY

"Those who have succeeded at anything and don't mention luck are kidding themselves"

Larry King, American TV host

Luck plays a vital role in all sports. Even the best golfers in the world would admit that there is a large slice of fortune involved in hitting a hole-in-one on a championship course. Sure, their superior skill means they are more likely to ace a par-3 than us mere mortals, but anybody who can hit the ball 150 yards or so has a chance of achieving the feat. In football, a high proportion of goals scored — more than 40% according to some analysts — involve some element of luck. And in cricket, the toss of a coin — effectively determining which team bats first — often has a disproportionate impact on the result.

Genuine incidences of good and bad luck affect every team and every player in every match. It helps to explain why a reasonable golfer can outperform an excellent one over 18 holes, why a good football team can lose to a lesser one and why a highly skilled bowler can fail to pick up any wickets in a match. By implication, sporting competition should *not* be considered a conclusive test of relative abilities…which is actually very good news! After all, without the influence of luck and other random factors, there would be little or no point watching two unevenly matched teams compete against each other. The result would be a foregone conclusion. Or put another way, one team must be hugely better than the other for the result to be certain.

The psychology of luck

We have all watched football games where a team dominates a patently inferior opposition but unluckily fails to score, before conceding a last-minute goal. This illustrates one way in which luck operates, influencing outcomes in completely unpredictable ways. But it has another, less direct, impact: a psychological one. You may have noticed a tendency in others or even yourself to attribute successes to skill and failures to bad luck! Take Thomas Frank, Brentford FC's former manager, for example. When asked how close his team was to perfection against Manchester City in a Premier League match in February 2024, he responded:

"*I think we were perfect. We were just unlucky.*"

Although Brentford only lost 1-0, the team conceded 11 shots on target, registering just two of their own. Manchester City's xG (expected goals) was 2.45, compared with Brentford's 0.35, suggesting that if any team was unfortunate, it wasn't the one from London.

This asymmetric approach — labelled Self-Serving

Bias — is an example of how System 1 instinctively acts to protect our self-esteem. Failing because of bad luck is less psychologically painful than failing because we performed poorly, while ascribing success to skill is more emotionally uplifting than putting it down to good fortune.

Four questions arise. First, why do we instinctively feel the need to rationalise events? Second, what is it about luck that makes it the perfect candidate to be ignored and invoked in equal measure? Third, does it matter that we use luck in the ways we do? Fourth, what is a better way to react?

1. Why we rationalise (badly)

Being human brings with it an instinctive requirement to understand the world and to make sense of what is going on around us. As we attempt to do so, System 1 ensures that we seek and accept 'causal stories' — those that explain how and why events have unfolded as they have — even in circumstances where there is nothing meaningful to understand or it is too complex for us to fully comprehend.

By wanting to accept such stories, particularly those that suit our case, it is easy to make mistakes. A case in point is our tendency to believe that, within reason, when two things are correlated, one must have caused the other. If a cricket team suddenly starts winning having swapped numbers four and five around in the batting order, for example, you can bet your bottom dollar that the upswing will be attributed to the switch, particularly if no other obvious changes have been made.

We find a concurrence of events *without* causal explanation — the definition of coincidence — psychologically unsettling, conflicting as it does with our inherent need for more tangible answers. We also have no idea how to conceptualise the likelihood of coincidences, the classic example being the 'birthday paradox.' Have you ever attended an event and discovered that two of the invitees, one of whom maybe yourself, share the same birthday? While there is a one in 365 chance of two people that meet at random being born on the same day in the same month of the year, the probability of a mutual birthday rises to 50% if we put just 23 individuals in the same room and to 99.9% if there are 75 in the room. These numbers may seem incredible, but only because we have little or no concept of how many different combinations of two people there are within a group of 23. It is 253 by the way.

It is hard to overemphasise just how common this tendency to underplay coincidences and search for causal narratives is. How many times have you heard somebody forcefully argue that their team won purely because of a single, skill-related factor such as an inspired substitution, a slight tweak to the formation or the ability of one player? Quite a few, I would venture and yet numerous factors — including luck — were far more likely to be at play.

2. Why luck is the perfect candidate

Consider the following:

- Is it unlucky to hit the goal post when attempting to score or simply the result of an inaccurate shot?
- Is it bad luck that your team's best player is out of action or the failure of the sports science department to ensure they are less injury prone?
- Is it lucky for a batter to miss a ball that they might easily have edged to the wicketkeeper or skilful of them not to nick it?

These sorts of issues could be debated for hours without resolution. The point being that it is often very tricky to differentiate luck from skill or the lack thereof. If somebody references bad luck for failure or skill for success it may be impossible to prove otherwise. The argument is emphasised by two well known, contrasting quotes about luck. The first, usually attributed to the legendary golfer Gary Player, is "The more I practise, the luckier I get," implying that what appears to be good luck is really the result of skill, honed through hours of practice. Meanwhile, Frank A. Clark, the American lawyer and politician, argued that "It's hard to detect good luck – it looks so much like something you've earned," suggesting the complete opposite.

But what if a team wins or loses, say, three consecutive matches? Luck cannot be the determining factor…can it?

An underappreciated aspect of random processes, including luck, is that they frequently deliver what *appear* to be systematic results. If we toss an unbiased coin a hundred times, seemingly non-random patterns are likely to emerge. It may be that we see ten heads in a row, or five tails followed by five heads. In such cases, not many would suggest that this is the result of skill. But they may well convince themselves of such if a previously poor team doesn't concede a goal for a couple of matches or a bad batter scores a half-century out of the blue. The team and batter *might* have turned a corner, but the sample size is nowhere near large enough to be sure. The same goes for a previously successful team and batter that suddenly does badly in successive matches. It could reflect a serious loss of form or just a run of bad luck.

What if the margin by which a team wins or loses is unusually large?

Again, luck may be heavily involved. In his book '*Fooled by Randomness*,'[1] Nassim Taleb makes the argument that the larger the deviation from the norm — the more a team/player out or underperforms their peers — the greater the chance that it reflects luck rather than skill. Every now and again, for example, we see a Premier League football team beating an opponent in the same league by a six or seven goal margin, but I wouldn't bet on it happening twice in a row, just I wouldn't bet on the losing team being defeated by the same margin next time out.

When Daniel Kahneman was asked by the online magazine '*Edge*' to report his favourite equation, he proffered the following:

Success = talent + luck

Great Success = a little more talent + a lot of luck

The message being that while most highly successful people are a bit better than their competitors, they are also likely to have enjoyed an unusual amount of good fortune. Correspondingly, an atypical quantity of misfortune may go a long way to explaining why somebody has endured significant failure.

There are, of course, individuals or teams that have proved themselves exceptions to this rule over the course of their careers — the likes of Tiger Woods, Pelé and Sir Don Bradman for instance — but the point is that they are so unusual that they have become household names as a result. Manchester United's longest serving manager Sir Alex Ferguson is another on the list and one that illustrates that legends also require plenty of luck. Having failed to win a major trophy in his first three seasons at the club and following a run of eight games without a win in late-1989, Ferguson was in deep trouble. The accepted wisdom is that he would have been sacked had the team lost to

Nottingham Forest in the FA Cup on 7 January 1990. It didn't, thanks to a Mark Robins goal in the 56th minute. The rest, of course, is history.

3. Why it matters

"So what?" you might ask. Does it really matter if we use and abuse luck to suit our purposes? In many situations, the answer is "yes."

By attributing success incorrectly to skill (not good luck) it is very easy to believe it will continue ad infinitum. Practice could be scaled back on the basis that "talent always shines through," players may be bought purely because their Key Performance Indicators (KPIs) have improved in recent times and bets are likely to be placed on false premises. In short, complacency creeps in, increasing the chances of mistakes and bad performances in the future.

The effects are similar when attributing underwhelming performances and results to bad luck. By letting ourselves off the hook, we might feel emotionally better in the short term, but will probably make the same errors again, potentially ensuring that failure becomes the norm.

It is particularly common to hear gamblers complaining about their misfortune when they have lost bets. Some will respond by giving up, perhaps claiming that they are just unlucky by nature, but others will persist on the basis that their luck is bound to change. This is a dangerous strategy to pursue given that luck may have had nothing to do with their losses, and even if it did, there is no way of telling when it will turn.

Whichever way you look at it, it is clear that self-serving bias discourages the search for improvement in sport: an essential ingredient, I would suggest, for sustained success.

4. What to do

The best way of countering the bias is to make a habit of conducting as honest an appraisal of performances as possible. This should be done following both defeat *and* victory. Indeed, there are often just as many lessons to be learnt from winning as there are from losing, particularly in closely fought games where a metaphorical toss of a coin effectively determined who took the spoils. This doesn't mean that perfection should be sought, partly because it is unobtainable and will add undue pressure — a single error ensuring failure. A much better idea is to identify a couple of areas of improvement, set achievable targets, and practise appropriately.

From an emotional perspective, it is often said that the best reaction to winning is not to get "too high" and to losing, "too low." To remain level-headed in other words. This is far easier said than done, however. Sport is full of emotions and, I would argue, all the better for it. As such, it is rarely good practice to hold post-match appraisals immediately after the game has finished. Waiting until emotions have died down is far more likely to bring productive conclusions.

When it comes to gambling, we should never risk our hard-earned cash on the basis that we are due a change in fortune. If making money is the key aim — as opposed to adding interest to the watching of games or 'hedging' emotions by betting against the result that would give us most joy — then we must strive to be as objective as possible. This means side-stepping self-serving bias as well as many of those biases detailed in the next two chapters.

One individual who would disagree with most of what I have suggested here is Brendon McCullum, pioneering head coach of the England men's cricket team. Following a massive 434 run defeat against India in the third Test of a five-match series in February 2024 — England's second biggest runs defeat since they started playing Test cricket more than 1,000 matches previously — McCullum was asked whether he analyses what went wrong. His response was:

"No, not really because that opens the opportunity for a) noise and also b) regret.... From a group point of view we try and turn the page pretty quickly and move on to the next opportunity...If you don't, you can often get stuck in past failures...we will just turn our attention to the next one and try and keep the health and confidence within the group high."

If true, it indicates that he believes the risk of players beating themselves up by reviewing mistakes is greater than the potential benefits of learning from them. I would have thought that there is a balance to be struck here. Post-match appraisals can surely be constructive not critical, while they needn't be overly lengthy.

For the record, England lost the next two Test matches, going down 4-1 in the series overall. This is not to suggest that the team would have won if they had chosen to review their mistakes. But England's recurring problems against spin bowling on turning pitches does suggest the current approach is failing. It is a subject I will return to later in the book.

Other consequences

There are other more light-hearted consequences of misunderstanding the role played by luck in driving outcomes.

It is interesting to observe, for example, how winning 'Manager of the Month,' or appearing on the front cover of '*Sports Illustrated*,' classically heralds a period of poor results. This is not because those that triumph are cursed, as some would have us believe, but because their success is often partly attributable to a run of good fortune that came to an end, something statisticians refer to as 'Mean Reversion.' Note how often a lesser-known golfer leads after the first round of a Major only to fall away in subsequent rounds. Yes, the pressure may have got to them, but more likely their opening 18 holes involved an unusual dollop of good fortune.

Mean reversion can also explain the so-called 'commentator's curse' whereby a confident prediction made by a sports commentator or expert is proved wrong almost immediately. Examples of such statements include sentences to the effect of "I can't see this team ever conceding a goal," "There's no way this bowler is going to take a wicket," and "I would be amazed if he putted this." The prediction is typically a simple extrapolation of recent events, the issue being that those events have often been shaped by (good or bad) fortune. When the luck turns, what appears to be a seemingly predictable pattern suddenly vanishes, to the embarrassment of those suggesting that it is bound to continue.

The most intriguing aspect of the causality-correlation confusion I referred to earlier is the bizarre rituals and superstitions that it gives rise to, even amongst the (seemingly) most rational of people. Supporters don their 'lucky pants' when watching their team play because that's what they wore when their team previously won; cricketers notoriously won't leave their seats if teammates look as though they are batting them to victory; footballers make a point of putting their left boot on before the right or vice versa and so on. I even caught my son, a Wycombe Wanderers FC supporter, carefully hanging a replica Wycombe 2020 Play-Off Final shirt in the car before driving to a League 1 home match against their opponents on both occasions, Oxford. While Wycombe won the Final 2-1, they drew nil-nil on this occasion.

Never mind that the opposing supporters/players do the same sort of things. To the extent that this possibility is even considered, it is probably only to conclude that "My lucky pants will be luckier than theirs." And if the ritual happens to fail, devotees usually blame themselves for getting some aspect of it wrong rather than conclude that the ritual itself had no impact.

How widespread is this behaviour? The only sports related study I came across when researching this question was based on a sample of 83 students, aged between 18 and 25, from Visva-Bharati University in India[2]. Published in 2022, it found that a staggering 82% of male athletes and 62% of female athletes competing at university level were of the view that "superstitious ritual behaviour is effective in sports performance enhancement" either "sometimes" or "often." Funnily enough, the same research also concluded that "Statistical analysis does not reveal any significant relationship between superstitious ritual behaviour and its effectiveness in sport performance enhancement." That is, it had no effect.

More generally, 34% of Britons (43% women and 24% men) described themselves as either "very" or "somewhat" superstitious, according to a 2023 YouGov survey. For interest's sake, the most widely believed superstition was that touching wood brought good luck (33%), while 14% even thought that getting pooed on by a bird was lucky! Proof, in my view, that if enough people say something sufficiently frequently, many will end up believing it.

Believe in luck

So far, I have focused on how we misuse the concept of luck for our immediate psychological benefit but longer-term disadvantage. There is another way, however, in which our thoughts about luck could influence performances. It is suggested that the simple act of believing that we are inherently lucky or unlucky will make us more/less successful than we would otherwise be. This may seem ridiculous but bear with me here.

Convincing ourselves that we enjoy an unusual amount of good or bad luck, *doesn't* mean we actually experience more or less good fortune. Rather, powerful psychological effects stem from the beliefs themselves. Those that truly believe that they are lucky are likely to take greater risks, be less anxious, and have a generally more positive mindset — all of which make winning more likely — than those convinced that they are unlucky. Numerous studies have shown that feelings of optimism and hope are associated with more favourable outcomes than pessimism and gloom.

On top of this, the Dysexecutive Luck Hypothesis proposes that by thinking of ourselves as unfortunate, we experience lower levels of 'executive functioning,' a set of cognitive skills that allows us to set goals, plan, regulate our emotions, concentrate, control our impulses and prioritise tasks. In so doing, our problem-solving and decision-making abilities deteriorate. We will achieve less than we are capable of achieving purely because we believe that we are unlucky. Correspondingly, if we consider ourselves lucky then we are more likely to utilise our cognitive skills to the full, improving our chances of success.

The hypothesis has received empirical support from several studies[3] and is potentially highly relevant when it comes to sport. After all, every sport is packed with problems to solve and decisions to make, both on and off the field.

There is a saying in sport that "good players have good luck." It is perhaps more accurate to say that "good players believe in good luck." Equally, we might blame bad luck for a defeat, when really it was our anticipation of bad luck that contributed to the loss.

A word on destiny

Another word that crops up frequently in the context of sport is 'destiny.' You will have heard people say things such as "It was my destiny to win the trophy," "I was destined to succeed" or "Destiny determined that I would lose." For some, a person's destiny is deemed to be in their own control, at least to an extent. For others, it is an entirely external force that operates in the same way as fate, meaning events are pre-determined in some way by a higher power. Of interest here, is why people connected with sport would believe the latter, effectively ceding control over part of their future.

The answer rests with an earlier observation: our necessity to explain events, preferably without relying on either coincidences or random factors producing apparently non-random outcomes. Not only are we disinclined to ascribe outcomes to these factors, but we instinctively assume that most events stem from somebody or something undertaking an action to achieve a particular purpose. If, out of the corner of our eye, we see a ball moving towards us, we naturally assume it must be because somebody deliberately kicked or threw it in our direction, for example.

A joint paper by Yale University's Konika Banerjee and Paul Bloom[4] proposed that viewing the world in these terms — which they describe as 'Agency, Purpose and Design' — is a cognitive bias that helps account for our reliance on fate/destiny. In circumstances where we are struggling for alternative explanations, fate or destiny are unconsciously considered to be reasonable concepts to invoke. If, for example, the best player in our team suffers a serious knee injury while warming up for a key match, we might say it was fate that ensured we lost the game. Others may be highly sceptical about this, but they can't prove that we are wrong. I find it fascinating how every year the Grand National winning horse is deemed destined to have triumphed. After all, there is always a great backstory behind its victory. The thing is we forget that *every* horse in the race has a great backstory, be it in relation to itself, the jockey or owner.

The other potentially helpful aspect of destiny is that by relying on it, we can release pressure on ourselves to always make the correct decisions and have the right answers. By absolving ourselves of responsibility for how the future unfolds, it allows us to feel better about relinquishing control. Sports men and women are always told by psychologists to focus on "controlling the controllables," but it is often left up to them to determine exactly what is and what isn't controllable. Sometimes they have a vested interest in pushing the future into the uncontrollable or 'destiny' column. The potential downside, of course, is that they are then left unprepared for it.

In brief

Self-serving bias ensures that luck generally has a bigger role in explaining success and a smaller part in explaining failure than we typically assume. While this System 1 cognitive predisposition represents a brilliant way of promoting self-esteem, it means that we are inclined to become complacent when we succeed and miss the opportunity to learn from mistakes when we fail. Performance levels are lower than they could be as a result.

The best way to counter the bias is to make a habit of conducting an honest assessment of our performance once emotions from the game have abated. Win, lose or draw, the key question should always be "how can I improve?"

Ironically, one way of doing so is to believe that we are lucky. While genuine incidences of good and bad luck are, by definition, entirely random and hence uncontrollable, thinking ourselves as lucky means we are more likely to fully engage with the task at hand in a positive manner than if we determine that we are unlucky. An important message of this chapter and others in the book is that it is often highly beneficial to fool ourselves into thinking in particular ways. By playing such mental games we boost our chances of success.

3
JUDGEMENTS AND DECISIONS

"The goal shouldn't be to make the perfect decision every time but to make less bad decisions than everyone else"

Spencer Fraseur, Author

When listening to people talking about sport, I am often struck by the wide-ranging views they have and how strongly they hold them. It is usually clear within a couple of minutes of sporting chat that they have formed strong opinions about a range of players, managers and teams, sometimes across a variety of different sports. But if you ask them why they have the perceptions they do, much umming and ahing typically ensues. In other words, we can be utterly convinced of our own case, often to the extent that we'll cling on to it in the face of overwhelming evidence to the contrary, without really knowing why! The same can be true even when large sums of money are involved. Explanations might be fuller in these circumstances, but make no mistake, hundreds, thousands or even millions of pounds are frequently put at stake on the flimsiest of judgement calls.

Chelsea FC's recent recruitment policy, described by Rory Smith of '*The Athletic*' as "dangerous" and "fundamentally stupid" appears to be a case in point. Just over two years after the club's ownership changed hands, Chelsea had spent a staggering £1.1 billion on 40 new players, hundreds of millions of pounds more than any other club in world football. The result? Chelsea finished sixth in the 2023/24 Premier League season, precisely unchanged from 2021/22, before moving up to fourth place in 2024/25. The last time the club won a *major* trophy was in 2021. Sure, all clubs are fallible when it comes to transfer market dealings, but the sheer number of players involved and the lack of a credible underlying strategy points to little more than a scatter gun approach in Chelsea's case.

As I mentioned in chapter 1, our capacity to form judgements and reach decisions in the blink of an eye is innate, bringing crucial advantages in highly time-sensitive circumstances, including many sporting ones. A batter facing a rock-hard cricket ball hurtling towards them at 90mph would be unwise to think too deeply about the situation, while the same is true of a footballer looking to score in open play when surrounded by defenders.

But there are plenty of sporting situations when a more considered approach would be beneficial. Determining which player from a range of potential transfer targets is the most suitable, how much we should read into a one-off result and what we should expect from a new manager are all examples where it would be useful to engage System 2. Even in these situations, however, our default is to rely on mental shortcuts — heuristics — that minimise the use of our mental resources and keep them engaged for the shortest possible time.

This chapter explores some of the many ways in which

we instinctively arrive at judgements in sport; how they are so often biased; what lies behind our strong attachment to them and what we can do to improve our decision-making.

How we judge…

Emotions

Most obviously, our assessment of players and teams is heavily influenced by whether we support them or not. We naturally tend to inflate the abilities of those we favour and vice versa for those we dislike. We might end up believing that a particular player has scored more goals or kept a greater number of clean sheets than is really the case, for example, or subtract several runs from an opposing player's batting average, often without having the slightest notion that this is what we are doing. The bias — a form of Affect Heuristic — speaks to the power of emotions in driving many of our judgement calls. Instinctively, we prioritise feelings over facts, meaning the latter often go unresearched or ignored if they happen not to suit our purpose.

The Halo Effect works along equivalent lines. Once we determine that we like or dislike one aspect of a person or team, System 1 automatically extrapolates this conclusion to other aspects of them including those we haven't even observed. In effect, an initial positive impression quickly equates to "they can do nothing wrong" and a negative one to "nothing they do is right." Such holistic judgements are typically formed within seconds based on potentially unrepresentative incidents and then prove highly resistant to change. Even minutiae such as the colour of a player's kit or their hairstyle can unknowingly influence our wider judgement of that individual.

England men's Test cricket captain, Ben Stokes, is a

great example of a player who enjoys a halo effect, largely escaping criticism when he makes mistakes and enjoying praise when it is unwarranted. If he spills a catch, commentators suggest that "the background made it difficult for him to see the ball." If an opposition batter is caught it is often because of "great field placement by the captain" and if Stokes is out playing a reckless shot, it is because "he's sending a message to the dressing room." In the unusual event that somebody dares to pop their head above the parapet it is always in highly qualified terms. Take the BBC's Simon Mann, for instance. Commentating on a Stokes' blunder in a Test match against the West Indies in July 2024, he suggested that "for a brilliant fielder, Stokes actually drops quite a lot" (of catches)!

Comparisons

Have you tried judging the height of somebody with no point of reference? If so, you will know how tricky it is. Alternatively, you may have watched a game of children's football officiated by an adult and subsequently been surprised by how short the referee is when another adult stands close to them. The fact is that we instinctively judge peoples' height in relation to other people or things.

This judgement by comparison is not just relevant when it comes to determining how tall somebody is. It extends to virtually everything we come across, including in sport. I have set out three examples below.

1. *The World Cup effect*

Watching the early stages of a World Cup, it is easy to be blown away by the performance of a particular player only to be disappointed by their subsequent showing in later matches or their regular domestic league. The owners and staff of many a club have been fooled in this way, massively overspending on players as a consequence.

One of the unusual things about World Cups is that they frequently pitch a good team against a relatively poor one, making players within the good team *appear* to be much better than is really the case. This only becomes obvious when they come up against an opposition of the same or higher standard, which will generally be the case in domestic leagues or the latter stages of tournaments.

The distortion doesn't just apply to World Cups, of course. Any competition where a player/team comes up against another at a different level can distort judgements. I might give the impression of being half-decent cricketer if I was to play against a team of 8-year-olds, but most certainly wouldn't if I had to face a county-level bowler.

2. *The curse of legends*

When it comes to judging managers and coaches, we typically compare the team's performance under their watch with what has gone before. Most of the time this doesn't create any issues but there are occasions when it does.

Since Sir Alex Ferguson retired as manager of Manchester United in 2013, the club is now on to its tenth replacement (four of whom were effectively 'caretakers'). The main problem for his successors is that they find themselves competing against a legend and suffering by comparison. In his 27 years as 'The Gaffer', Sir Alex Ferguson won 38 trophies, including 13 Premier League Titles, five FA Cups and two UEFA Champions League: an astonishing legacy which has effectively raised expectations for all those that have followed.

Memories of the 27 years that preceded Ferguson's reign either don't exist or have faded in the case of older supporters, making a quick summary of interest. During that period, Manchester United's average finishing position in the top division of English football was between seventh and eighth. The team won the title just twice and were even relegated on one occasion. They scooped one European Cup (the equivalent of today's Champions League).

The combination of this history, Sir Alex's once in a generation abilities and the big improvements made by other clubs suggest that Manchester United shouldn't be expected to finish in the top four and/or win a Cup every season. Yet, failing to do so guarantees unrelenting criticism and a P45 for the latest incumbent of the managerial hot seat.

If you think that's bad, look at what has happened at Nottingham Forest, where the ghost of another managerial marvel, Brian Clough, continues to spook his replacements. In an incredible 18 years at the club, Clough took the team from the second tier of English football to the first, winning the League title, four League Cups and back-to-back European Cups. Since Clough left in 1993, Forest have run through 36 managers (including caretakers) and won nothing of significance, other than a couple of promotions back to the top division.

Similar effects are witnessed when it comes to individual players. If somebody is perceived to be replacing a star, comparisons will follow. It may be more then 50 years since Pelé stopped playing for the Brazilian national team, but anybody wearing his iconic Number 10 shirt is still compared by many with the footballing genius, to their detriment. This is obviously an extreme example, but judgements of these sorts occur at every level in every sport.

3. The Substitute Illusion

Isn't weird how a team's substitutes suddenly become a lot better when their colleagues are performing poorly? We convince ourselves that if they were playing rather than sitting on the side lines the game situation would be very different.

This is another comparison effect. In these circumstances, we *know* that the players on the pitch are doing badly, meaning those that are not actively participating seem to improve, albeit only relatively. They obviously don't get better in an absolute sense. We often confuse 'relative' with 'absolute,' the result being that if the replacements do enter the fray, they frequently disappoint. We forget that there is usually a performance-related reason why they are sitting on the bench in the first place.

It works the other way round as well: substitutes appear to get worse when their team is playing well. Managers are usually reluctant to change a winning team even when elements of it will, from an unbiased perspective, be improved by a replacement. It is often not until the weaknesses are exposed that an adjustment is made, by which time it is too late.

In similar vein, average batters magically morph into excellent ones as soon as they are joined in the middle by a poor batter: cricket being perhaps the only sport where professional players must engage in a discipline they are not very good at. Many bowlers are rotten batters. The consequence? It immediately feels as though it is all but impossible to get the average batter out and, indeed, the fielding team is usually happy to concede runs if it ensures the poor player is on strike. They effectively only seek the wicket of one batter not two as they would do if both players were of average quality.

Outcomes

Even more important than emotions and comparisons in shaping perceptions is the role played by outcomes. After all, what better way to determine the superior team or player than to look at results. If Manchester United beat Liverpool, Manchester United must have played better than Liverpool. And what's more, if Liverpool then defeat Arsenal, we can safely conclude that Manchester United are likely to outdo Arsenal. These judgements might appear to be entirely logical, but there is a good chance that they are flawed.

The fact is, one-off sporting outcomes are a far from perfect indicator of team quality and likely future performances. Sport allows for a team to play better than the opposition, sometimes significantly so, and still lose. In the previous chapter, I pointed out how luck affects results, but this is not the only disruptive influence. Poor officiating can distort outcomes independently of performance, while injuries, unusual lapses of concentration and ill-judged substitutions/team selections are some of the many reasons why a single match can be a poor indicator of a team's underlying abilities. No wonder season-long league competitions generally offer a far better guide to a team's (relative) standard than cup competitions where fewer matches are involved.

Although these arguments are well known and widely accepted, this doesn't stop us drawing and extrapolating conclusions from tiny samples. Such behaviour is more understandable when we don't have time to watch all relevant matches before deciding on the make-up of our Fantasy Team, for example. Pundits, however, have no such excuse and yet appear to be particularly prone to this phenomenon known as Outcome Bias. Unconventional cricket shots are described as "brilliant" when they result in a boundary, but "reckless" when the batter is out. They will often wax lyrical about a winning team's performance even though they played poorly and the opposing team deserved to win.

Just like the rest of us, most pundits read too much into the number of goals/runs/points scored and conceded in a single match. They overreact. Indeed, listening to some, it is easy to get the impression that if a team has been thrashed it will never win again, while the victor is henceforth unbeatable.

This is not to deny that goals/runs/points are important metrics in judging the quality of teams, they're just not as important as we think they are when viewed in small quantities.

WYSIATI

No, this is not a typo, but an acronym that stands for What You See Is All There is! Coined by Professor Kahneman, it represents yet another way in which the brain instinctively simplifies our lives. He points out that System 1 will always attempt to concoct stories from the information it has, even if that information is severely limited or unreliable.[1] The fact is we don't look for what we can't see and aren't fully aware of what we don't know. As an example, he suggested that if we are told that the leader of a country is intelligent and strong, we are highly likely to jump to the conclusion that the person is a good leader. We don't bother to think, let alone inquire, whether they might have weaknesses that haven't been mentioned. The addition of the word *corrupt* to the list of characteristics would immediately transform our conclusion.

It is also what lies behind a good chunk of the angst associated with social media. Seeing pictures of other people having fun, we automatically assume that they are always having fun, while we know that the same is not true of ourselves. Ironically, we then proceed to post pictures of ourselves having fun!

WYSIATI is relevant to many sporting judgements we make. Watch a highlights reel of virtually any player and we are almost bound to conclude that they are great, while the opposite is the case if all we view is their clangers. No doubt many a player has been bought on the basis of a series of carefully selected clips sent through by well-meaning agents! Even when scouts or data specialists provide contradictory evidence, it is hard to shake-off the impression left by a montage of memorable moments. It is only by watching the player in a full match that we realise that quite a lot of bad accompanies the good — what we previously saw is *not* all there is — and disappointment sets in.

I challenge anybody to watch Adama Traoré's 'Top Dribbles' on YouTube and *not* conclude that he is an incredible player that any team would want. By the end of the 2024/25 season, the 28-year-old Spanish winger had played 432 professional football matches, scoring just 35 goals, while assisting (a goal) on 67 occasions. This equates to a goal involvement every 4.2 games on average. If we look at his 247 Premier League appearances alone, the same statistic rises to just over 6 (14 goals, 25 assists). Traoré has played for five different clubs at senior level. By comparison, the less flamboyant Harvey Barnes has scored 49 goals and assisted 32 times in 200 Premier League matches for just two clubs– a goal involvement every 2.5 games. The total transfer fees they have commanded so far are almost identical.

Zak Crawley is cricket's equivalent to Adama Traoré. Look at his best shots, and you will be amazed that he only averages 31 for England in 98 Test match innings and 32 in 232 first class innings. Devotees of the Ashes will likely remember the fantastic four he scored from the first ball of the 2023 series in England, described as a "real statement" by Sky Sports' Michael Atherton at the time. Optimism soared, but England went on to lose the match.

Action Bias

Action Bias is an instinctive tendency to prefer action over inaction, even though there is no particularly good reason to act. In effect, we pay more attention to the benefits of acting than the disadvantages of doing so.

Some have argued that it represents a conditioned response as doing something is more likely to be rewarded by others than remaining passive. An evolutionary explanation has been proffered as well: running away at the slightest hint of danger, rather than sticking around to find out whether the situation really is hazardous, improved our chances of survival. Either way, it applies widely in sport. A good example is goalkeepers opting to dive rather than stand still when facing a penalty. Although research indicates they have a marginally higher chance of making a save by remaining where they are, it looks and feels better to be doing something.

Managerial sackings in professional football are another case in point. The average tenure of a Premier League manager is currently just over two years, while it was less than 16 months across Europe's top divisions last season. A manager whose team finds itself in the relegation zone or thereabouts is all but guaranteed to get the sack these days, even if the team was widely tipped to go down at the start of the season.

Whether this is a good thing for the club is a matter of contention. According to analysis from BBC Sport, published in December 2024, there have been 91 occasions a Premier League side has parted company with its manager when the team was in one of the bottom three places.[2] Of these, 36 avoided the drop, equating to a success rate of 40%. Pretty good you might think. We don't know, however, what would have happened if the original manager had remained in place.

A study by Sky Sports made a stab at this by examining periods following a sequence of poor results when the manager was *not* sacked.[3] It suggested that results often picked up. Referencing Arsene Wenger's 21-year reign at Arsenal as an example, the authors pointed out that every notable low in the team's results which could have seen him dismissed preceded a bounce in form. The reality is that a run of poor results can reflect any number of temporary and/or longer-lasting factors; factors that maybe beyond the ability of a new manager to sustainably fix. If so, any improvement in form is likely to be temporary, which is exactly what the study found to be the case in most situations:

"*On average results improve for the first six games after dismissing a manager, after which, results taper off and return to levels recorded nine games before the sacking.*"

And yet, most owners and/or Directors of Football clearly feel a compulsion to act when the team is doing badly, even though they were responsible for hiring the manager in the first place and will likely have to pay compensation to remove them. We might think that decision-makers should be strong enough to ignore pressure from fans baying for the manager's head, but they frequently aren't. Typically, they act in haste and then repent at leisure.

Stereotyping

Stereotyping — our instinctive categorisation of people into specific groups — is another way in which we form judgements without having to engage System 2. While it brings advantages, allowing us to instantly anticipate how certain individuals, groups of people or even nations are likely to behave in particular situations, mistakes are common in all sorts of areas. Again, sport is no exception.

See a particularly tall football player and we automatically think that they must be good in the air. Meanwhile, a short player is deemed likely to be poor when it comes to heading the ball. A player with a 'low centre of gravity' is bound to be a good dribbler, while a rangy one will be clumsy on the ball; an 'oversized' cricketer will hit the ball a long way, and a slight one won't; a small bowler is unlikely to bowl that quickly, but a muscular one will. At a national level, many of us unthinkingly assume that every Italian football team is good at defending, Brazil always plays beautiful football and England are terrible at penalties!

Depending on the level of sport involved, most stereotypes have a greater than 50% chance of being correct. But the question is, is it wise to act upon them without undertaking some research? It is entirely possible, of course, that a tall footballer is not a good header of the ball, that a slight cricketer does hit the ball long distances and that England wins a penalty shootout.

If the answer matters and we have time, we would probably all agree that a bit of homework is worth undertaking. Even so, many players are undoubtedly ignored simply because they don't look the part, while plenty who appear to fit the bill are selected when they shouldn't be. Perhaps England's penalty taking abilities have been underestimated as well in recent times!

…and why we won't let go

Having reached judgements and come to decisions, often in a fraction of a second, we typically form a bizarrely strong attachment to them. Sure, we all flip flop on occasion, rapidly shifting views depending on which way the tide is turning, but most of the time we hang on to them to the bitter end. Why?

Confirmation Bias provides part of the answer. Once we have concluded that a team, player or manager is good/bad we automatically favour evidence that supports that conclusion, while dismissing that which doesn't. In essence, we compare any new information with our belief and only store it if it fits with our existing view.

Let's assume that we watch a football match in which a player we rate highly is largely anonymous in the first half but does much better in the second. The chances are that we will give much greater credence to their second half performance and leave the game more convinced than ever that our view is correct. Alternatively, we could be a spectator at a T20 cricket match where a favoured player's bowling spell sees them serving up several 'hit me' balls, with some unplayable ones. Our dominant memory will be of the latter.

In both situations, if we had the opposite view to begin with, we would have reached precisely the opposite conclusion about their performance. This phenomenon, by the way, helps explain why two people watching the same event can arrive at completely different verdicts about the performance of the individual players or teams involved.

Confirmation bias is one way in which we avoid so-called Cognitive Dissonance: those mentally uneasy, slightly stressful, times when we are exposed to information that is inconsistent with our views. Rather than deal head-on with the apparent contradiction, which is uncomfortable, we opt to ignore it. Alternatively, we might rummage around social media, desperately seeking supportive statements from those who share our beliefs or come up with excuses for those episodes that don't fit our views.

There are social explanations for our reluctance to give in to contradictory evidence as well. Changing views can be considered a sign of weakness or disloyalty. Even when we have solid reasons for adjusting our stance, we can be deemed "too soft" to stick to our guns or "unfaithful" for doubting our favoured team's abilities. Being perceived to be talking up the opposition is a complete no-no as well. This illustrates the power of Social Norms: those unwritten rules of engagement we have when dealing with others. Having evolved as a social animal, we instinctively want to fit in, be part of a group, and if that means playing by the established rules, then play by the rules we do. Here, the rules are that we don't give in or think badly of our own team, even if this comes at the cost of more accurate judgements.

In a similar vein, being wrong about something once is embarrassing enough, but, for most of us, proving to be incorrect twice simply can't be countenanced. Clearly, the risk we run when publicly altering views is that our initial judgement turns out to be correct. We worry that being 'topped and tailed' in this fashion will lower our status within the groups we operate, with others thinking of us as foolish or worse. Such concerns are also highly relevant when it comes to adjusting predictions and unwinding bets, the subject of the next chapter.

How to respond

As human beings, we are all prone to odd thinking when taking decisions and making judgements. And while I would suggest that a degree of quirkiness is no bad thing, it is hard to make this case in situations where it reduces our chances of success, costs money and/or occupies valuable time as we attempt to undo mistakes. The question is, what can we do to improve our thinking?

I suggested earlier that the instinctive nature of most of our strange thoughts means that our options are limited. Yes, a greater awareness of our tendency to trade accuracy for speed and probability for plausibility might help, but it is often insufficient. I have a couple of other suggestions for those making important decisions.

While we can't help *thinking* impulsively, we needn't always *act* in this way. When decisions or judgements are important and we have time to consider the issue at hand, we should use that time. This is particularly crucial when an instant response springs to mind, irrespective of how right that thought initially seems to be. This doesn't mean waiting days or weeks but, if possible, we should sleep on the issue. Sleep can rid us of unhelpful emotions and allows our mind to sift through the various thoughts of the day. It is why we often wake up with greater clarity than we had the night before. While this is an obvious suggestion to make, I am equally aware that we don't do it often enough.

The use of data should be non-negotiable when it comes to many important decisions as well. Sure, data can mislead and be manipulated by those so inclined but, used appropriately, it provides greater objectivity than the human brain can achieve, bypassing cognitive biases and revealing insights that are otherwise easily missed. For example:

- A player who appears to be a great asset, perhaps because they are extremely skilful, may be found to have considerable weaknesses in other key areas.

- Somebody who runs in an unconventional way and is ignored by scouts as a result, could be faster than generally appreciated and have other strengths.

- A football team scoring a lot of goals might be significantly exceeding its xG, suggesting this period of success is unlikely to last.

- A ranking of players based on specific criteria will throw up names in an instant that (non-data) recruitment specialists are unlikely to have even considered.

In short, data analysis is an incredibly powerful tool but, as somebody famous once said, "With great power, comes great responsibility!" Users must always endeavour to be open-minded, not motivated by confirmation bias to prove a point.

When decisions are made collectively, it is critical to ward off Groupthink. This phenomenon stems from a reluctance to debate/dispute/argue for fear of upsetting others, often leading to poor-quality judgements. A social norm — the desire to avoid conflict — spills over into situations where it is disadvantageous for it to do so. We end up accepting things that we don't agree with because it represents the easier and less risky option. A possible solution is to set aside time to actively discuss the weaknesses of a decision and to consider what could go wrong. For it to work, the group leader must be willing to encourage a dialogue of this sort and receptive to what comes from it.

Notwithstanding these arguments, it is important to remember that there is no such thing as perfection when it comes to taking decisions. We don't have perfect foresight and there is not always a clear right and wrong choice to be made in any case. Our aim should be a far more modest one: to maximize our chances of making the best decisions possible.

A fascinating issue that arises in this context is whether the use of Artificial Intelligence (AI) systems — specifically Large Language Models (LLMs) — could help us achieve this goal. LLMs are already in widespread use, writing essays on behalf of no doubt grateful students, composing songs and writing code amongst many other things. Trained using enormous quantities of text scraped from the internet, LLMs are extremely adept at understanding, summarising, translating, generating and predicting text. But can they make 'good' decisions?

When I asked ChatGPT itself whether it could reach sporting decisions, the answer was:

"*I can certainly help analyse sports situations, discuss strategies, or suggest possible decisions based on available information. However, I don't make definitive sporting decisions like a coach or manager would.*"

At present and for the foreseeable future, LLMs require human input to make judgement calls fundamental to most decisions. A paper from OpenAI, the creator of ChatGPT, indicates LLMs can be taught to mimic human judgement (as determined by a small group of people) when it comes to various aspects of writing.[4] The models are then able to extrapolate what they have learnt to answer questions quite different from those originally provided, in the same style. According to researchers at the University of Toronto's Rotman School of Management, this explains ChatGPT's ability to produce higher quality text than that normally found on the internet from which it undertakes the vast bulk of its learning.[5]

So, if LLMs can judge the difference between 'good' and 'bad' writing, it seems plausible to suggest that it could be taught to use judgement in many other matters as well. An obvious problem would remain, however. Given the necessity for human involvement in the initial teaching stage, there is a good chance that many of the biases I have referred to in this chapter and elsewhere in the book will resurface in the judgement calls of the LLMs themselves. Additionally, the models are bound to have huge difficulties in dealing appropriately with people's individual, unpredictable preferences.

As such, it is hard to see LLMs markedly improving our decision-making abilities any time soon. Currently, the best they can do is provide us with a list of factors that we might consider in coming to decisions. These are potentially useful, although as far as I can tell, the cognitive biases we should look out for are never included. I suggest they should be.

In brief

With the best will in the world, errors of judgement and poor decisions are inevitable. Equally, however, we don't always help ourselves. Evolutionary forces mean we generally make decisions and come to judgements within a fraction of a second. While this is generally very useful, it can also cause problems.

There are a huge range of shortcuts our brain

automatically takes to reach judgements, all of which can create biases. Accurate judgements and good decision-making usually require emotions to be ignored. But System 1 elevates their status, ensuring we are overly positive about those we support and too negative about those we don't. We instinctively rely on lazy comparisons, which can frequently mislead, and read far too much into one-off results. We focus on easily accessible information, such as highlights packages, while ignoring information that is effortful to retrieve. We feel the pressure to act when it would be better to leave well alone. And, for the sake of simplicity, we stereotype players and teams, mentally allocating them to specific boxes that they don't necessarily fit.

Having formed views in these ways, other powerful psychological forces ensure that our inclination is to stick with them, often until all hope is lost and sometimes beyond! We generally deal with the mentally uncomfortable consequences of contradictory evidence by ignoring such information altogether, finding convenient excuses for its occurrence and/or seeking support from like-minded others. Social norms can also make it difficult for us to change our opinions, particularly if this involves being perceived as disloyal or giving in.

When something is important and we have time to consider our options we should use that time to think carefully. The appropriate use of data can also bring greater clarity and, with it, better decisions. Used well it cuts through views distorted by cognitive biases, bringing us closer to the truth. Large language models might help channel our thoughts in appropriate directions, but do little more than this right now.

4
PREDICTIONS AND PUNDITS

"The idea that the future is unpredictable is undermined everyday by the ease with which the past is explained"

Daniel Kahneman, Psychologist

Sport and predictions go hand in hand. We seemingly can't help but speculate about the results of sporting competition, while many of us go further, putting our money where our mouth is by betting on outcomes. The global sports betting market is currently worth around $100 billion and this doesn't take account of private wagers between two or more individuals. Two questions of psychological interest arise:

1. Why are we so keen to make sporting predictions?

2. Why are our sporting predictions so often wrong?!

Predictably predictive…

To understand our predilection for sporting forecasts, it is essential to understand why we are so keen to predict the future more generally. We wouldn't do so unless there were important benefits to be had and I have listed several of these below.

- Predictions allow us to prepare ourselves appropriately for future events, providing us with a degree of control over an uncertain future. During our long history as hunter-gatherers, uncertainty often spelt physical danger, making it essential to predict what might play out.

- It is only by making countless assumptions (predictions that we are almost certain will be fulfilled) that we are not lost in a mire of anxiety and unnecessary preparations for every possible eventuality.

- By comparing predictions with outcomes, we can learn what works and what doesn't, allowing us to adapt our approach if necessary.

- They provide an opportunity to be proved right! As well as benefiting our self-esteem, correct predictions may raise our social status and help others who heed our advice.

With these factors in mind, it is not hard to see why making predictions has become such an instinctive (System 1) process. Now, as we go about our daily lives, we formulate forecasts about almost everything, including sporting outcomes, mostly without any conscious thought whatsoever.

On top of this, we believe that making predictions is

far easier than it is, encouraging us to continue doing so. Part of the reason is that accurate forecasts stick in our mind far longer than our inaccurate ones, a function of confirmation bias. We are also naturally inclined to focus on how situations panned out in reality, while forgetting about all those scenarios that we thought might occur but didn't. So-called Hindsight Bias has the advantage of leaving our mind less cluttered than it would otherwise be, but means that we perceive past events as more predictable than they were before they took place.

Finally, we shouldn't forget that predicting results offers the possibility not only of being proved correct but receiving a financial reward as well. There are few things in life that bring more joy than that! In fact, the feeling can be so alluring that it becomes addictive, the problem being that it can also prove agonisingly elusive at times.

...but too easily wrong

Unfortunately, and despite plenty of practice, most of us don't have a particularly good record when it comes to forecasting sporting outcomes. In some ways this is unsurprising. Barring successful time travellers, nobody has or will have perfect foresight. Apart from anything else, genuine incidences of luck often determine results and luck, by definition, is randomly distributed.

Nevertheless, we could and should do better. As highlighted in the previous chapter, we make a lot of mistakes that could be avoided simply by pausing for thought. I want to elaborate on some of those here as well as examining the reasons behind other common forecasting blunders.

One thing we habitually do when making predictions is extrapolate recent trends without thinking enough about the reasons behind them. Put another way, we are predisposed to think that when a player or team has gained momentum (both upwards and downwards), there is little or nothing that will stop it. If Fulham have won two games in a row, for example, we are more prone to think that they will win a third than we should be. By engaging System 2, we might decide that their success reflected a new manager bounce, or that the opposition teams were missing key players. If we conclude this to be the case, then the value is probably in taking the opposite view. Momentum can be illusory.

We also have a penchant for predicting what we *want* to happen or believe *should* occur, as opposed to what is most likely to play out. This ensures that we are overly optimistic when it comes to predicting the results of teams we support and too pessimistic about those we dislike. Equally, we might favour a team because they deserve to win, rather than impartially judging which team is likely to perform best.

This effect, termed Optimistic Bias, is most obvious when it comes to national competitions, with England's run to the 2018 football World Cup semi-final a perfect case study.

In the group stage, England beat Tunisia and Panama but lost to Belgium. This was enough to see the team through to the last 16, where they defeated Columbia on penalties, before beating Sweden in the quarters. By the time of the semi-final against Croatia, the overwhelming majority of my compatriots were convinced that, "Football was coming home!"

There were, however, several reasons not to be quite so optimistic. The team's performances had, to that point, left a lot to be desired; Croatia was performing much better; England had only played one top ten ranked team in progressing to the semis (Belgium) and lost; and both France and Belgium (the other semi-finalists) were evidently superior teams.

Nevertheless, even Mark Lawrenson — a former Liverpool player and BBC pundit who represented the Republic of Ireland at international level — became caught up in the tide of enthusiasm. Speaking ahead of the Croatia match he said:

"I just have a feeling that England will find a way to win. Sometimes I think these things are written – and the way this tournament has opened up for England is one of the reasons it feels like this is their time…While England's results have been a lot better than their performances, that is not a bad thing in a tournament like this."

Clearly, any attempt to provide rational analysis had long since evaporated. More interestingly the betting odds — which partly reflect the relative weight of money placed on the possible outcomes — saw England priced at 11/8 to triumph in normal time (a bet of £8 providing a profit of £11 if successful) and Croatia at 13/5. This equates to a 42% probability of England winning in 90 minutes and just 28% for Croatia. It was also notable that English players dominated the list of those considered most likely to score the first goal. "Nobody to score" in normal time was deemed more likely than Croatia's most prolific striker. As it turned out, England were first to score (although the goal came from an unfancied player), but the team still lost 2-1.

This is not to suggest that England were bound to lose but rather that the odds almost certainly reflected a lot of nationalistic betting. Of course, many Croatians may also have been betting on their team for the same reason, but given the relative sizes of the two populations, I suspect those that did were heavily outnumbered.

Recency Bias skews our predictions as well, leading us to attach too much importance to recent events, experiences or information. As most memories fade over time, it becomes increasingly effortful to retrieve them, meaning we are incentivised to rely on those that are comparatively fresh. Waning memories can also make us feel as though the actual event happened longer ago than it actually did.

In July 2024, it took just one good performance by England cricketers Gus Atkinson and Shoaib Bashir in the first and second Test matches respectively against a poor West Indies side for several ex-England players to declare both as world-beaters. Their inferior records at county level weren't considered worthy of any airtime whatsoever. Sure, they may turn out to be extremely successful, but history is littered with players (from all sports) who have been lauded as the next big thing in the immediate aftermath of an excellent but atypical performance, only to disappear from sight a few months down the line.

This heuristic further explains why we rarely predict a change in trend even when that trend is not well established. If a team has played badly in recent times, we find it very hard to conceive of them playing well and vice versa. All that springs to mind when thinking about the future are poor performances. And yet sport, indeed life in general, is full of ups and downs.

Another phenomenon that intrigues me about football specifically is the excitement generated by the awarding of corners and free kicks in dangerous positions. When a crowd is present, you can literally hear the rising expectations of a goal, while watching hundreds of people setting up their phones to record the seemingly inevitable moment of triumph.

But consider this. In men's professional football, most studies find that for every 100 corners taken, 97 do *not* end in a goal. This means that the probability of a team scoring from each corner kick is roughly 0.03 (3%) or, put another way, a team that averages five corners a game is only likely to register one goal every six to seven games from this source.

When it comes to scoring directly from a free kick, assuming a shot at goal is taken, the probability is higher, but only modestly so at about 0.05 (5%) in men's football. In the English Premier League, which began in 1992, David Beckham holds the record for the highest number of goals scored from free kicks. No shocks there. You may, however, be surprised to know that his tally is only 18 (from 265 Premier League appearances). Meanwhile, every time West Ham's James Ward-Prowse steps up to take a direct free kick the commentator is guaranteed to make some mention of his expertise in this department. He is second in the rankings having scored 17 (from 404 appearances). That's one every 24 games, implying a good season will see him register two such goals.

So, what's going on here? Why do we repeatedly predict something that is very unlikely to happen?

The answer lies partly with Availability Bias. Not surprisingly, our recall of emotionally charged events is much better than it is for the humdrum of everyday life meaning that we overemphasise the frequency of the former and understate the latter. While English football followers of a certain vintage will recollect *that* goal scored by David Beckham against Greece in 2001, ensuring England's passage to the World Cup Finals, we have forgotten about all those free kicks where he failed to find the net. I would wager that every time he took a free kick thereafter, the image of his Wembley goal flashed across the minds of TV viewers, spectators and players alike. Everybody expected him to repeat the feat when, in reality, the chances of him doing so were tiny.

The (English men's) cricketing equivalent is Ben

Stokes' heroics in the 2019 One-Day World Cup Final in 2019, where he made an unbeaten 84 and a further eight runs in the Super Over. No matter that he enjoyed a sizeable chunk of luck that day, what we remember is his extraordinary talent in incredibly challenging circumstances…which we then expect him to replicate every time he comes to the crease or gets the ball in his hand. Stokes has backed up this success on a couple of subsequent occasions, but the truth is he has failed far more often than he has succeeded. Many forget that he bowled England's final over in the 2016 T20 World Cup final, conceding four consecutive sixes from four very hittable deliveries. England lost the match, having been firm favourite to win it before that over commenced.

The Possibility Effect is also influential here. As part of their groundbreaking Prospect Theory, Daniel Kahneman and Amos Tversky demonstrated that we assign much greater significance than we should to possible but unlikely events given the emotions they trigger. The (small) chance of something good happening, can provoke intense feelings of hope and excitement.

In a later study based on a series of psychological experiments, the same authors quantified the 'perceived' probability we attach to outcomes at different 'true' probabilities. I have replicated their results on the next page.[1]

While the data tells us that if our team wins a free kick or corner, it only has about a 3-5% chance of scoring, it feels about three times more likely than that.

Now think about penalties, where the true probability of scoring is 75-80%: it is likely, but not certain, to result in a goal. In this case, Kahneman's and Tversky's results suggest that we expect it to lead to a goal just 60% of the time. In other words, if we want the team to score, we are more concerned than we should be that it won't. This is termed the Certainty Effect and, again, reflects the influence emotions have on decision-making. The comparatively small chance of a penalty miss weighs heavily — we can't help worrying about it — affecting our implicit prediction.

True Probability %	Perceived Probability %
0	0
1	5.5
5	13.2
20	26.1
50	42.1
80	60.1
95	79.3
99	91.2
100	100

Likewise, if a very good team is playing a very bad one and we care about the result, we implicitly attach a smaller probability to the former winning and a higher probability to the latter than is warranted. Our predictions are biased, meaning that what may appear to be attractive betting odds for the underdog, and unappealing as far as the favourite is concerned, are no such thing. Put another way, we bet too much on possible but unlikely outcomes and too little on likely but not certain events. It helps to explain why betting companies love to offer accumulators and why we love to accept them.

Should we trust our gut?

It is often suggested that when facing uncertainty, we should go with our gut feeling, our inner voice if you like. But should we really heed such advice and trust our gut?

We all experience gut feelings: that strong, sometimes overwhelming, sense that something is bound to happen. Seemingly, we can see the future. It is very common amongst followers of sport where countless predictions, many of which are translated into bets, are based on this apparent psychic ability of ours. In truth, there is nothing psychic about it at all.

Gut feelings are simply a physical manifestation of a prediction generated by System 1. It feels mysterious because our conscious mind is not involved in the process. Rather it is a function of our intuition and therefore little more than the result of recollections of past experiences that our brain has — rightly or wrongly — concluded resembles the current one. The prediction may turn out to be correct, but then again it may not.

Social scientists argue that intuition works best as a predictive tool when two conditions are met. First, there is a regularity to events, meaning that history *does* repeat itself. Second, there is an opportunity to learn those regularities through prolonged practice. Professor Kahneman points to chess as the best example of a "regular environment," while also suggesting that firefighters and physicians "face complex but fundamentally orderly situations." The situation facing stock pickers and forecasters of political developments in democratic countries is very different, according to Kahneman. In these instances, the past represents a far from perfect guide.

Unfortunately, most worthwhile sporting predictions fall into the same realm as stock picking and political forecasting. Having acquired a basic knowledge of the sport and players involved, our ability to predict results is unlikely to improve (and may get worse – see below) by watching, say, 10,000 games. Malcom Gladwell's oft-quoted mantra that it takes 10,000 hours to become an expert doesn't apply to forecasting sporting outcomes, even when System 1 insists otherwise.[2]

The bottom line? While we should listen to what our intuition is telling us, we shouldn't accept its conclusions without conscious (System 2) inquiry when the prediction matters.

Do pundits know better?

Many years ago I was watching an English Football League (EFL) cup match between Manchester United and Middlesbrough, when the audio link to the commentator at the ground went down. The studio experts were called upon to perform the role themselves with illuminating results. Rather than simply describing what was happening in the same way as a professional commentator would or suggesting what was likely to be going through the players' minds based on their own experiences, they proceeded to predict the outcome of each penalty and even, in a couple of cases, which side of the goalkeeper the ball would be struck. They also did this while forcibly arguing that penalties were a complete lottery! It didn't end well for them…or indeed Manchester United for that matter.

As well as illustrating the principle that people — including those who should know better — can't stop themselves making predictions, the experience made clear that pundits are just as bad as the rest of us when it comes to the accuracy of their forecasts. My example only involves penalties in a single match, but more thorough examinations generally tell the same story.

Take the BBC's football prediction game. Here, former Premier League striker turned pundit, Chris Sutton, is pitted against the general public (in the form of those who can be bothered to participate) as well as different guest celebrities. All are asked to submit their prediction for every Premier League and FA Cup match each week, with the results reported on the BBC website. In the 2023/24 season, Chris beat the 'Guests' — many of which, it should be noted, made attention-seeking predictions — but lost to the rest of us. To be fair, he did at least exact revenge in 2024/25.

Meanwhile, the BBC's 30 football pundits (yes, 30) were asked to predict the Premier League top four at the start of the 2024/25 season. Not one, thought Liverpool would triumph, while only two placed them second. Tottenham and Manchester United were the fourth and fifth most fancied teams to finish in the top 4, ending the season in 17th and 15th places respectively. Just one pundit correctly forecast that Manchester City would not finish either first or second.

We shouldn't be shocked. Finance industry research has shown that experts' forecasts are consistently worse than those with less knowledge! I strongly suspect that this is true of most sporting pundits as well. Not only are they subject to the same cognitive biases as the rest of us, but they tend to be overconfident to boot. Kahneman notes that we shouldn't trust experts simply because they sound confident:

"*Declarations of high confidence mainly tell you that an individual has constructed a coherent story in his mind, not necessarily that the story is true.*"

This tallies with my own experience as an economist working in financial markets for more than 20 years. The most handsomely rewarded professionals were usually the ones that could spin the best yarns in the most confident manner. Yet their forecasting record was almost certainly inferior to their less confident colleagues.

The panel of BBC TV pundits wheeled out to cover

the final of the UEFA European Football Championship in 2024 provided another excellent example of why it is unwise to trust the predictions of sporting experts. Asked to provide their pre-match forecasts, the English pundits unanimously predicted an English victory based on shaky arguments not dissimilar to those used by Mark Lawrenson that I quoted earlier. While the England team had performed poorly to date, it was "bound to click at some point." Sure, Spain had played the best football in the tournament to that point, but England had "world class" attacking players.

In the aftermath of the Spanish victory and without reference to their previous predictions, the pundits then confidently delivered detailed analysis of Spain's qualities and England's failings, all of which had already been crystal clear in each of the six matches played by both teams preceding the final.

It seems to me that the only purpose of asking pundits for their predictions is to allow viewers to make fun of them when they are proved wrong or, even worse, to hail them as gurus if they happen to be right!

This is not to say that all pundits are superfluous. While they may be unable to provide anything other than amusement value when it comes to making predictions, they *should* be capable of communicating valuable insights gleaned from their personal experiences–experiences that the rest of us don't have. These could be tactical, psychological or physical; anything that helps us understand and enjoy the sport to a greater extent.

Seeking improvement

So, if we can't trust pundits or rely on gut feelings, how can we improve our sporting predictions?

For most of us, it is enough just to be more aware of

the role cognitive biases can play in affecting our sporting predictions and respond accordingly. For others, more drastic action will be required, which, as with many other decisions and judgements, will almost certainly involve the use of data.

The analysis needn't be that complex. Numerous studies, including in sport, have demonstrated that even the simplest of formulas can yield more accurate results than top of the head predictions. The task is also made easier by the quantity of data now publicly available for most sports. It is no coincidence that the most successful betting advisory companies don't ignore data but squeeze every last drop from it.

Even then, however, plenty of uncertainty is bound to remain. To reiterate an earlier point: perfect foresight is unobtainable. Things happen in sport that nobody can hope to predict however much data is used. The most we can do is improve our probability of success, not guarantee it.

In brief

Our unconscious mind generates predictions all the time and, in so doing, is heavily influenced by the cognitive biases I have described both here and in the previous chapter. We extrapolate recent trends without thinking enough about the reasons behind them; we predict what we want to happen as opposed to what is most likely to play out; we rely too much on our memories, which recency and availability biases distort; we overestimate the probability of possible but unlikely events and underestimate the chances of highly likely but not certain events.

Pundits are subject to the same biases as the rest of us and are just as likely, if not more, to make poor quality predictions. Trusting gut feelings is no guarantee of success either. They are simply indicating that our unconscious mind has recognised a situation similar to one that has occurred in the past. It may or not play out in the way it did previously.

Eliminating as many cognitive biases from our predictions as possible — something which is most likely to be achieved through the responsible use of data — is a sure-fire way of improving our forecasting abilities.

5
FORM AND 'THE ZONE'

"When you have confidence, you can have a lot of fun. And when you have fun, you can do amazing things"

Joe Namath, former American football quarterback

There are many peculiarities relating to form (defined as a player's performance relative to their normal or average performance). The following are a few examples:

- Some players play consistently well against a particular opponent, but poorly against another of an equivalent level.
- Players perform at a high level in one competition but badly in another.
- A long-lasting winning streak can give way to a sustained losing streak and vice versa.
- Players sometimes rediscover form in the middle of a game.
- Teams can perform consistently better playing *away* from home than they do playing at home.

In some cases, as we saw earlier, luck explains such apparent peculiarities. Just as we can toss an unbiased coin ten times and get ten heads, a player or team can win or lose ten evenly contested consecutive games as a result of a run of good or bad fortune.

Technical factors may also be important. There is, for example, a big difference between the nature of red and white ball cricket: the latter involving a limited number of overs, fielding restrictions and, crucially, pitches and balls that generally provide less movement, making it easier to hit through the line of the ball. The technique of some players is better suited to one form of the game than the other.

The nature of pitches varies *within* the red and white ball game as well. Wickets in the sub-continent are usually low and slow, favouring the spinners, while those in Australia are fast and bouncy, aiding the quicks. Seam bowlers tend to outperform in the UK. Bowling conditions can even vary during a match as the pitch wears and the weather varies. In a four- or five-day game, a wicket that was seamer-friendly to begin with, can 'flatten out' before offering significant help to spin and/or reverse swing bowlers.

But this is far from the full story. The mental side of sport — the way we think about it — has highly influential effects on performance. This was illustrated perfectly by Rory McIlroy, just the sixth man to complete golf's career Grand Slam. Speaking after his long-awaited victory in the 2025 Masters, he explained:

"I have always had the physical attributes to be able to get the job done. But I think it was the mental hurdle I needed to get over."

A whole academic community and entire industry have sprung up to examine how thoughts can sway outcomes and help athletes get the most from their mind.

Sport psychologists point to a myriad of channels through which thoughts affect performance. These include determining how confident we feel, our level of concentration, how anxious we are, our resilience to setbacks and our degree of motivation. We can probably all agree that a player who believes in themselves, who is able to focus on the task at hand and who is feeling calm and motivated will outperform somebody of equivalent ability who is experiencing none of these things.

What is less clear, however, is what determines players' thoughts in these areas and the mechanisms by which they influence sporting performance. It is these issues that I will focus on here.

1. Thought drivers

Every training session, every game and (virtually) every situation within a game will trigger a Schema within the minds of all those involved, which in turn influences what they think and feel about it.

Schemas are best described as a mental framework that helps organise, process and store information about people, places, objects and events. Their purpose is to save time, supplying us with a package of information — effectively a simple, mental impression of how situations are likely to develop — that varies depending on the circumstances we face. The precise make-up of that package is largely determined by instinct, our own previous experiences and learnings from others. All schemas are stored in System 1 with the relevant one activated automatically.

To illustrate how they work, let's start with a non-sporting example. Assume three people are on a walk together when they come across a dog. Person One's 'dog schema' incorporates their own positive experiences of owning a dog when they were younger: as such they might talk and pet the dog. In contrast, Person Two's schema is full of fear and mistrust because they were chased by one when they were a child: they back off. Person Three also feels anxious because they were told by their parents that most dogs bite and should be avoided: they too keep a safe distance away. Here, the same dog triggers three different schemas and two different reactions.

Schemas work in the same way when it comes to sporting situations. Say, Player One is due to face their arch nemesis, Player Two, somebody who intimidates them. Even though the former has worked on their game and improved significantly since the last time the two played each other, their schema, as it relates to the forthcoming match, incorporates a lot of negativity. They feel anxious and full of self-doubt.

Perhaps a batter is due to come up against a team they scored a hundred against on two previous occasions. Their schema will be filled with positivity. They remember what it felt like to play so well; how easy they found it to score runs. The playing conditions may be more challenging this time, but they start their innings brimming with confidence. In contrast, the bowlers' schemas might incorporate images of being hit frequently to the boundary and feelings of inadequacy.

What if a player was badly injured the last time they competed at a particular venue? Coming back to that venue, even several years later, may trigger memories of the pain they felt and the long, boring period of subsequent recuperation. They worry that history will repeat itself and feel reluctant to fully commit to the match. Their reaction contrasts with teammates and opponents who haven't experienced the same thing.

Schemas are not necessarily set in stone. It is possible

that subsequent experiences lead to an adjustment or even a complete reversal in the nature of the schema. As a rule of thumb, the more extreme the experience, particularly in relation to the emotions it evoked, the more resistant the schema will be to change. A schema that incorporates a particularly bad defeat, great performance or horrific injury is more likely to remain in place than one where the defeat was narrow, the performance average or the injury a minor one.

The development of schemas and their potential adjustment all happen at an unconscious level. We don't become aware of the thoughts and feelings they contain until they are triggered, at which time we generally accept them as factual representations. Most of us don't question our schemas or, if we do, struggle to counter any negative thoughts they yield with more constructive versions.

2. How thoughts affect performance

There are several ways in which the thoughts and feelings within schemas influence performance.

Motivation

Let's start by assuming that two different competitions trigger two contrasting schemas in a player's mind. In the first, they feel highly motivated to do well, perhaps because it is of higher kudos, while they are not so bothered about the second. As a result, they try harder and concentrate more in the former, which in turn elevates their probability of success in that competition relative to the other. This assumes that their opponents don't think in the same way, of course.

Comparative levels of motivation can make all the difference in a game of fine margins, while it is also highly relevant when it comes to local derbies and other fierce rivalries. What one team lacks in technique can sometimes be made up by an overwhelming desire to beat their rivals. It may help explain why Manchester United has (generally) performed surprisingly well against Liverpool in recent times and why Scotland has such a good record against England at a national level.

Anxiety

It is also easy to see how anxiety-ridden schemas could impact sporting performance. Players might focus too much on *not* making a mistake, *not* getting injured or *not* being sent-off, holding back in key moments of the game. They may overthink as well, concentrating on the mechanics of a sporting action, rather than relying on muscle memory alone. I suspect this is what lies behind the yips: a sudden inability to execute specific sporting skills, such as putting or throwing darts.

These issues hit the sporting headlines when the superstar US gymnast, Simone Biles withdrew from the Tokyo Olympics in 2021, saying that she was "having a little bit of the twisties" — the gymnastic equivalent of the yips which causes a person to lose their sense of space and dimension when in the air. Reacting to the news, ex-gymnast Catherine Burns described the phenomenon as follows:

"*You're moving way too fast, you're totally lost, you're trying to think but you know you don't usually think to do these manoeuvres, you just feel them and do them.*"

Having taken a break from the sport, Biles returned to compete in the 2024 Paris Olympics, brilliantly winning three golds and a silver. Sadly, many others haven't been so lucky.

Resilience

How players' performances are impacted by setbacks will depend heavily on their degree of mental resilience. The future performances of less resilient players will suffer when they lose, while those of high resilience players could even improve. In the case of the former, defeat leads to a period of navel gazing, infighting or other destructive pursuits, while the latter focus their thoughts and energies on more constructive activities such as what they can do better next time.

In this way, two players of equal physical and technical ability, but opposing mental attitudes toward disappointment, might see their performances move in opposite directions after a couple of defeats.

Confidence

It is generally agreed that the closely related concepts of confidence, belief and expectations have a significant bearing on performance. They often prove to be self-fulfilling. It is no exaggeration to say that schemas that incorporate low confidence, a lack of self-belief and defeatist expectations all but guarantee failure, while ones that embody a healthy level of confidence, strong self-belief and optimistic expectations significantly improve the chances of success.

Roger Bannister's achievement in breaking the supposedly insurmountable 4-minute mile barrier is the classic example of the power of self-belief, partly in relation to his own success, but, more importantly, what followed it. As if by magic, several other top athletes suddenly managed to do the same thing having previously fallen short. Knowing that a sub-4-minute mile was humanly possible created the belief amongst those athletes that they too could achieve the feat, tipping the balance in their favour.

What about Leicester City's fairytale triumph in scooping the 2015/16 Premier League title? Having only just avoided relegation the previous season, bookmakers gave the team a 5000-1 chance of finishing first. To put this in perspective: victory for The Foxes was deemed far more *unlikely* than the Loch Ness monster being found (500-1), Alien life being discovered (1000-1), or Elvis Presley being alive (2000-1)!

A multitude of explanations have been proposed for what must be *the* most improbable success story in sport. Surging confidence following a good start to the season is prominent amongst them. According to Matt Reeves, Head of Fitness and Conditioning at Leicester at the time:

"*In the early part of the season results went in our favour; we fought back from behind several times and scored a number of late goals. This built confidence amongst the squad and helped to establish a winning mindset among the players…Confidence and momentum were key, as was togetherness between players and staff.*"

The experience of Alex Hales, the Nottinghamshire batter, is another great example of how confidence matters. Back in 2015, Hales was picked to play for the England Test match (red ball) team in a four-match series away against South Africa, before featuring in five one-day (white ball) internationals against the same opposition. Having scored just 136 runs at an average of 17 in his eight Test match innings, he then proceeded to score 383 runs at an average of 77 in the one-day matches, becoming the highest scoring English batsman ever in a five match ODI series. Patently, his form turned in the most dramatic of fashions.

This partly reflected his better technique against the white ball. But I would wager that when thinking about batting again in the ODIs his thoughts were overwhelmingly confident ones, while his red ball schema was very different. Hales now only plays white ball cricket having announced his retirement from the shorter forms of the game in 2018.

A lack of confidence or an erosion thereof can have equally dramatic effects, Arsenal's loss to Manchester City in the 2022/23 Premier League title race being a prime example. As City's form improved in the new year, Arsenal's began to fall away. For no obvious physical or technical reasons, the Gunners' near invincibility evaporated as the finishing line approached and City won match after match. A similar course of events has unfolded over several seasons now, such that it is no doubt embedded within the schemas of players from both teams (as well as the rest of us). They anticipate the season panning out in this way, making it more likely that it will.

So far, so clear. What is less apparent, however, are the exact ways in which confidence, belief and expectations affect performance?

To answer this question, it is useful to begin with the concept of placebos. 'Invented' in the 1770s they can be defined as 'fake' medicines or procedures designed to fool the recipient into believing that they are receiving genuine treatment.

Professor Robert Buckman, a clinical oncologist, argued:

"*Placebos are extraordinary drugs. They seem to have some effect on almost every symptom known to mankind, and work in at least a third of patients and sometimes in up to 60%. They have no serious side-effects and cannot be given in overdose. In short, they hold the prize for the most adaptable, protean, effective, safe and cheap drugs in the World's pharmacopeia.*"

For more than two centuries, nobody could comprehend how something with no active ingredients could have such dramatic effects. But the relatively recent advent of brain imaging technology has shed light on this. If we *genuinely* expect our health to improve, the chemical make-up of our brain changes in the exact same ways as it would if we were actually experiencing better health. Stress hormones drop, while dopamine levels and endorphins rise, the impact of which is to enhance mood, motivation and concentration, while reducing the perception of pain and promoting a greater sense of well-being. Even the efficacy of our immune system may benefit.

Not surprisingly, nocebos – treatments that are anticipated to harm, usually via adverse side-effects – have the opposite impact. We feel worse having taken them. Experts argue that nocebos have a larger detrimental effect on clinical outcomes than placebos, as negative perceptions are formed much faster than positive ones. I will discuss the reasons behind this in chapter 7.

The use of placebos is no longer isolated to the medical profession but widely deployed in other areas, including sport. Examples of sporting placebos include dietary supplements, creams, cupping and inert injections, the administration of which is designed to boost the confidence of players. Players expect to perform better as a result. Again, most research studies have found placebos (and nocebos) to be impactful in sport: a systematic review of 20 such investigations concluding that "The pooled effect size for placebo effects was moderate to large," while "based on five measures from three studies, the nocebo effects were almost twice as large."[1]

It is precisely by stimulating the chemical changes described above that placebos and nocebos can improve/worsen sporting performance. In the case of placebos, players will feel more motivated to perform, less inhibited by anxiety and better able to focus. Thoughts won't wander (so often) in unhelpful directions such as the possibility of defeat or, for that matter, the spoils of victory. By feeling better about themselves, players should also enjoy greater resilience–the odd defeat or poor performance being less likely to drag them down. All in all, it is hard to think of a better tonic for sports men and women, or, correspondingly, anything worse for players who succumb to nocebos.

Of course, expecting pills, supplements and the like to have an impact is one thing — after all, we are conditioned to anticipate effects from 'medical' treatment — but can the same positive and negative consequences of placebos and nocebos be triggered in other ways? In short, "yes."

I very much doubt, for instance, that the high-profile examples of confidence effects I have just referred to involved the widespread use of physical placebos and nocebos. At a more mundane level, we have all witnessed (and probably experienced) how a favourable couple of results can transform confidence, creating genuine expectations of future success which translates into positive thoughts, feelings and actions. And correspondingly, how one or two losses undermine self-belief, in turn contributing to further losses. The only thing that matters is that the expectations are authentic. Players must genuinely believe that they will succeed or fail for the chemical balance within the brain to change. System 1 — our unconscious — can't necessarily tell the difference between what is real and imagined. It can be fooled.

There are two further observations to make about confidence and its effect on performance. First, it can prove extremely fickle and fragile, very easily gained and lost. Football teams that are playing badly and losing by a couple of goals can suddenly gain confidence when scoring even the most fortunate of goals. A cricket team that is piling on the runs often panics when a couple of wickets go down in quick succession or crumble when facing scoreboard pressure. A bugbear of mine has been teams' (not least England's) preference to bat second in white ball matches. How many times have we seen players' form desert them under pressure of trying to chase a 'par' score, let alone a high one? This is particularly apparent towards the end of major competitions.

The England football team's extraordinary loss to Iceland in the last 16 of Euro 2016 also illustrates the brittle nature of confidence in pressure situations. England took an early lead from the penalty spot, but Iceland equalised almost immediately and then went in front in the 18th minute thanks to a goalkeeping howler. England's confidence visibly collapsed, such that they couldn't complete even the simplest of passes as the game progressed. Defeat became inevitable, while Iceland became the smallest country by population (336,000 – roughly the size of the city of Coventry) to reach the quarter-finals of the competition.

Second, players can become *overconfident* usually after a series of wins or because they perceive the opposition to be inferior. Here, the benefits of the chemical changes referred to are more than offset by negative effects such as a tendency to underprepare, make silly mistakes and fail to learn from errors.

Overconfidence no doubt helps explains the many Cup shocks — whereby a lower league team beats a higher league one — that occur. We have also seen it at times during McCullum's and Stokes' reign as head coach and captain respectively of the English Test match cricket team. I referred previously to the chastening 434 run defeat England suffered at the hands of India in early 2024. As India piled on the runs England's opening batter Ben Duckett was asked how many runs the team would be comfortable chasing. His memorable response was:

"The more the better…this team is all about doing special things and creating history. They can have as many as they want and we'll go and get them."

England were all out for 122!

The psychology of form

We are now ready to circle back to the example peculiarities of form I started this chapter with and which I have reproduced below. I have added short, (theoretical) psychological explanations for each of the phenomena based on the ideas discussed in the chapter.

- *Some players play consistently well against a particular opponent but poorly against another of similar standard.* The player's schema for the two opponents is very different. The first is full of confident thoughts, which stimulate helpful changes in brain chemistry, making victory more likely, and the second the opposite. The former stems from a convincing victory against the opponent at youth level many years ago and the latter from feelings of physical intimation.

- *Players perform at a high level in one competition, but badly in another.* They have contrasting levels of motivation for the two competitions, not matched by their opponents. They have (wrongly) come to believe that one is associated with good luck and the other with bad luck. As such, they try hard in the former and don't put so much effort into the latter. They win the first and lose the second, seemingly reinforcing their views.

- *A long-lasting winning streak can give way to a sustained losing streak and vice versa.* Having won several games in a row, the players become overconfident, believing that they are unbeatable. They fail to train properly, losing a couple of matches which they wrongly blame on factors outside of their control. The losing sequence continues, testing their resilience, until the penny finally drops: they have let standards decline and need to work hard to get back to where they were.

- *Players sometimes rediscover form in the middle of a game.* A player starts the game feeling a bit rusty having been unable to train adequately in recent days. They make a couple of mistakes but then something goes right, something they associate with good performances in the past. They feel a surge in confidence and their performance improves.

- *Players can perform consistently better when playing away from home than at home.* A player has begun to feel the pressure of expectation from home supporters having done well in recent matches. They now feel anxious when playing at home, worrying about failing rather than focussing fully on the match itself. Their schema for away matches is more helpful. They are able to shut out the noise of the crowd and concentrate on performing to the best of their ability.

'The Zone'

A particularly intriguing aspect of form that I haven't touched upon yet is 'The Zone,' also known as Flow. It is a term that lacks a formal, generally accepted definition, but I would use to portray those occasional episodes in sport when a player performs so far from the norm (in a positive sense) that on-lookers are left in a state of near disbelief. It should be stressed that being in The Zone doesn't guarantee success — the opposition, amongst other things, will have a say in this — but it does significantly improve the probability of achieving something special.

From the players perspective, it is described as a state of supreme focus that helps them perform to their full potential. Such is their level of concentration that the passing of time and other potential distractions, both internal and external, go unnoticed. It can be likened to a trance-like state.

Plenty of research designed to identify the factors behind what is the holy grail of sporting mindsets has been conducted over the years. And while it must all be taken with a pinch of salt, partly because of the difficulties in precisely pinpointing episodes of Flow, the results are worth a peek.

Having investigated 17 studies of relevance, academics from the Panteion University of Social and Political Science in Athens concluded that:

"Athletes who are engaged, committed, confident and able to perceive challenges as opportunities rather than threats, are more likely to experience flow. Links between confidence and other correlates can emphasize its empowering effect."[2]

They noted that the various studies had found confidence to be linked to "mental toughness," the "absence of negative thoughts and emotions," "optimal arousal," "effective practice and preparation," and "commitment," amongst other things. It is not made clear whether confidence generates these features or vice versa — I suspect that the causality runs both ways — but the point is that, by hook or by crook, players must feel highly assured. This is very least that is required to be in The Zone.

Other research, not specifically focussed on sport but still of relevance, has identified the sort of situations in which Flow is most likely to occur. According to Professor David Melnikoff of the Stanford Graduate School of Business and fellow researchers, the task must be perceived as neither routine nor unreachable but somewhere in between. Participants must be uncertain about the outcome, highly motivated to reduce that uncertainty and aware that they can do so through their own repeated, increasingly successful efforts.

He provides the example of a virtuoso and a novice both seeking to play a piece of music flawlessly on the piano. Since the former is certain that they will do so and the latter is equally certain they won't, neither will enjoy Flow. Instead:

'For flow, we believe someone should feel like, 'I might nail this, or I might flounder. Let's find out.''[3]

The fascinating aspect of this work is that it points to a more nuanced role for confidence in stimulating Flow. Players should be sufficiently confident to believe that a difficult task is achievable, but not so confident that they perceive it to be straightforward. If they then add a large dollop of intrinsic motivation, a high degree of technical ability and plenty of determination they will give themselves the best chance of entering The Zone. Anxiety should be absent, of course.

Such a psychological state must then be accompanied by the right external environment, which is where uncontrollables — such as playing conditions, the performance of teammates, the nature of the opposition and luck — come in. All in all, a lot of different things need to come together at the same time for Flow to occur and brilliance to emerge. It is why Flow, according to my relatively strict definition, is rarely witnessed, making it all the more special when it is.

Can sports psychologists make a difference?

The difference between the thoughts I have discussed in this chapter and those in the previous ones is that the former are deemed (more) controllable. If correct, the implication is that sportspeople can be trained to think in ways that will enhance their performance, giving them an edge over opponents who focus solely on the physical and technical aspects of their sport.

At a professional level, this is generally the job of sports psychologists. By encouraging the use of techniques including self-talk, visualisation, goal setting, breathing and other relaxation exercises, positive body language and even the selection of appropriate music, their aim is to ensure that athletes' minds work for rather than against them.

But are their interventions effective? Can athletes learn to think more constructively? An analysis of numerous studies researching this issue concluded:

"Overall, sport psychology interventions hypothesized to enhance performance were shown to have a moderate beneficial effect, whereas variables hypothesized to be detrimental to performance had a small negative effect."[4]

I would interpret this as a tentative yes, which I suspect would be a far stronger one if everybody using psychological techniques spent time perfecting them and, for the reasons discussed, fully believed in their efficacy.

Rory McIlroy is one that has done so, reaping considerable rewards as a result. Ex-golfer and pundit, Paul McGinley said of McIlroy's sports psychologist, Bob Rotella:

"He's becoming an increasingly louder voice in his (McIlroy's) ear with massive credibility, because of the guys that he's got over the line. To have somebody in his ear that he really respects, that makes things simple for him, that gets things refocussed and re-energised, is absolutely crucial."

In brief

The vagaries of form often reflect the way players think about sporting situations. Such thoughts and their associated feelings — usually packaged together in a mental schema — stem from instinct, relevant personal experiences and lessons from elsewhere. This means that two players of equal ability can react very differently to the same situation.

The mechanisms by which thoughts affect performance are many and varied. They directly determine a player's motivation, how anxious they feel and their degree of mental resilience, all of which are key drivers of success. They also dictate confidence, the most important psychological influence of all in this context but also the least understood…until recently. By genuinely expecting something (good or bad) to occur, our brain chemistry alters in ways that improve the probability of that something playing out. Thoughts can be self-fulfilling.

A high level of confidence is a pre-requisite to being in The Zone, although it shouldn't be so high that we believe our objective to be straightforward. Plenty of other ingredients, not all of which are controllable, also need to come together at exactly the right time for magical performances to materialise. This is what ensures that episodes of true Flow are rare and likely to remain so.

Sports psychologists can help athletes obtain and retain form using various techniques. To be fully effective they require belief in their benefits and plenty of practice.

6
REFEREE AND UMPIRE BIAS

"Referees are only human, I think"

Phil Kearns, former Australian Rugby Union captain

In November 2024, the UK's sporting headlines were dominated by highly derogatory comments from Premier League referee David Coote about Liverpool and its then manager, Jürgen Klopp. The remarks were delivered three or four years previously in a video that was made public for reasons unknown.

When asked on Sky Sports whether the video would fuel the belief amongst fans that certain referees have an agenda against their club, ex referee Dermot Gallagher commented:

"*I have refereed for 46 years, and I think most of my decisions are based on what I call instinct. You have a knowledge of the laws of the game, you have the experience you have built up over them years. You see an incident and you act instinctively on it….So I don't think any referee has a chance to think about things like that.*"

Clearly, Gallagher was either unaware of the unconscious cognitive biases outlined in this book and elsewhere, which, if true, would represent a remarkable failing, or he conveniently forgot about them. As human beings, all match officials are subject to the same instinctive biases as the rest of us; the only question being are they any better at *not* acting upon them. Luckily, plenty of research has been conducted to investigate the issue.

Home bias

In football, the most obvious potential bias concerns the influence of fans on referees–the theory being that match officials will be kinder to home than away teams to appease the (generally) far higher number of home supporters.

It is widely accepted that Home Advantage exists, but its causes have been the subject of much debate. Aside from having fewer supporters at the ground, away teams must contend with less familiar surroundings as well as the wearying effects of greater travel. Some clubs also go out of their way to make the away dressing room as uncomfortable as possible. Leicester City's opponents, for example, are met with a tiny changing room that gratuitously incorporates a false pillar in the middle, while Norwich City famously painted the away changing room a deep shade of pink. The hope was that this would promote feelings of kindness and compassion towards the home team!

Not many good things came from the appalling global pandemic, but it did at least provide the perfect opportunity to isolate and test for a fan-effect given that most leagues banned supporters part way through the 2019/20 season and for almost the entirety of the 2020/21 season. The best such study was conducted by four academics from the Universities of Leeds and Northumbria who compared referee decisions as well as team performance across 4,844 games — 3,515 with crowds and 1,329 without — from 15 Leagues in 11 countries during the 2019/20 season.[1] They found significant differences between the two periods.

Before COVID-19 struck, teams earned an average of 0.39 more points per game at home than away, scoring an additional 0.29 goals than the opposition in the process. These figures all but halved to 0.22 and 0.15 respectively once spectators were absent, pointing to a sizeable fan-effect of nearly 0.2 points a game.

The same analysis was not conducted for 2020/21, but suffice to say something remarkable happened in England that season. For the first time ever, away teams registered a *higher* number of average points per game (1.43) than home teams (1.36) in the country's top division. In other words, home advantage completely evaporated. And what's more, this didn't reflect the results of only a handful of teams. Of the League's 20 participants, 11 scored more points away than at home in the season as a whole.

What happened when crowds returned in full in the 2022/23 Premier League season? Home Advantage resumed in earnest, with home points per game rising to an average of 1.68 and away points dropping to 1.09: a gap of 0.59 points. Just one team — Southampton — scored more points away than at home. In the subsequent season, the points gap between home and away teams narrowed, but was still a substantial 0.41, with Burnley the only exception this time.

At face value, these figures indicate the fan-effect in the Premier League is worth something in the order of 0.5 points per game to the home team – a massive impact – and can explain home advantage in its entirety. Interestingly, other European leagues didn't see home advantage wholly removed when fans were absent in the 2020/21 season, suggesting either that the fan-effect is bigger in the Premier League or a statistical oddity of some sort was partly responsible for the extraordinary events of that English season.

Nevertheless, whichever way you look at it and whatever major league you examine, fans do influence results. The next question is how. To what extent can the fan-effect be attributed to referee bias as opposed to the psychological influence crowds have on player performance?

The most direct measure of the pressure exerted by supporters on match officials is provided by referees' disciplinary judgements. The same study of the 2019/20 season referenced above showed that before COVID struck, referees awarded more fouls against the away team than the home team, whereas the numbers were almost identical thereafter. The same story also applied to both yellow and red cards, with away teams seeing a notable drop in those handed to them during the COVID period.

Taken in isolation, this strongly suggests that referees are biased in favour of home teams when fans are present. But the authors pointed out that the change in referees' behaviour could, at least partly, have reflected the more even nature of matches during COVID. Bearing in mind that defensive actions tend to be associated with more fouls and cards than attacking ones, away teams were likely to have been penalised less because they were defending less. Once taking account of this, the fan-effect on red cards became statistically insignificant, although it remained robust in the case of both fouls and yellow cards.

Disciplinary actions are not the only way in which referees can favour home teams. Professor Dr. Thomas Dohmen of Maastricht University in the Netherlands tested whether they benefited disproportionally from stoppage time decisions and decisions to award goals and penalty kicks.[2] He did so by looking at more than 3,500 games from Germany's top division — the Bundesliga — with the matches taking place between 1992/93 and 2003/04.

The findings were illuminating. He found that referees awarded more stoppage time at the end of the second half "when the home team is one goal behind, than in matches in which the home team is one goal ahead." Meanwhile, "when one team is ahead by two goals or more, the amount of stoppage time does not depend on the identity of the leading team and less time is added." Under these circumstances, of course, the outcome of the match is all but certain. Professor Dohmen estimated the additional time given to home teams when they were losing narrowly averaged 22 seconds, which, as he pointed out, was actually a lot less than the remarkable 113 seconds provided in Spain's La Liga according to another study. We shouldn't forget that, according to legendary manager Brian Clough, "it only takes a second to score a goal."

Professor Dohmen also discovered that the distance of the crowd from the pitch made a sizeable difference to the amount of extra time added in Germany. In stadia where fans were close to the pitch it amounted to almost one minute when the home team was losing narrowly, whereas when a running track separated the stands from the pitch, there was no such home bias.

What about goals and penalty kicks? Here, Professor Dohmen uncovered further evidence of home advantage:

- 5.0% of (non-penalty) goals scored by the home team were incorrectly awarded, according to data from IMP AG, the official provider of statistics for the German league. This compares with 4.0% of goals scored by the visiting team–a statistically significant difference. The home team was particularly likely to be falsely granted a goal if it was losing narrowly.

- 35% of penalties given to the home team shouldn't have been awarded, while the equivalent figure for the away side was 27%–again, a statistically significant gap. Referees were 10% less likely to accurately award a penalty kick in stadia without a running track.

- The visiting team was wrongly denied a legitimate penalty in 36% of cases compared with 30% in the case of the home team.

In short, Dohmen's results suggest that the bigger the imbalance between the number of home and away fans and the closer the fans are to the pitch, the more referees are likely to favour the home team by providing extra time, allowing non-penalty goals and awarding penalty kicks. This is particularly true of match situations where the home team is losing narrowly. Fascinating!

Reputational bias

It is often said that referees tend to favour larger, more successful clubs: think Manchester United, particularly during Sir Alex Ferguson's reign, for example. If true, this may also reflect a fan-effect, when it comes to home matches at least: bigger clubs generally having bigger stadiums which accommodate a greater number of home supporters. But could there more to it than this?

A study of referee behaviour in the Norwegian Premier League (NPL) indicated that there may well be.[3] NPL matches have the 'advantage' of relatively low attendances — an average of less than 7,000 in 2024, compared with more than 38,000 in the English Premier League and nearly 40,000 in the Bundesliga — meaning fan-effects are likely to be smaller. Indeed, the research was unable to detect any evidence of referee bias towards home teams.

With this in mind, the main part of the study saw an Expert Panel of four Norwegian Premier League referees evaluate 43 potential penalties involving either Rosenborg or Molde — deemed to be the country's two most "impactful" clubs, "based on their status and previous success." The detailed clips of each situation were stopped before it was possible to identify the referee's decision, while the audio was muted and the time and score information was hidden.

Of the 43 incidents, the match referee awarded 11 penalties to Rosenborg and Molde, whereas the expert panel concluded that they should have been awarded ten. Not a big difference there. But when it came to their opponents, just one penalty was given, while the panel thought eight should have been awarded. The authors concluded that "referees' decisions may be unintentionally biased by a team's success."

Correspondingly, there is evidence to suggest that referees are biased against 'underdogs.' This is according to a 2007 research paper which found that such teams are on the receiving end of more disciplinary sanctions than favourites.[4] Perhaps ex-Wolverhampton Wanderers boss Gary O'Neil was on to something therefore, when, following a controversial last gasp goal against his team in October 2024, he said:

"*There's no chance that people are purposely against Wolves. But is there something in the subconscious around decision-making or, without even knowing it, are you more likely to give it to Manchester City than Wolves?...I've spoken to them (PGMOL) about this as well, and they obviously guarantee me there isn't.* (But) *They are human.*"

Needless to say, O'Neil was asked to explain himself to the FA, no doubt receiving a slap on the wrist for raising a perfectly legitimate and important issue.

What about referees' reactions to teams widely considered to be particularly aggressive or 'dirty?'

This effect was investigated in 2002 by researchers from Staffordshire University, who randomly assigned 38 referees officiating in semi-professional or professional matches to either an experimental or control group.[5] The two groups were then presented with the same 50 video clips of incidents from football games, all involving a team in blue, and then required to indicate what action they would take. Those in the experimental group were informed that the blue team had a reputation for foul and aggressive play, while the control group was not.

Beforehand, five highly experienced referees allocated the events into three groups – those that they all agreed were fouls (labelled 'certain' incidents), those where they disagreed ('uncertain' incidents) and those that they unanimously accepted were not fouls ('innocuous' incidents). All of them were committed either by or against the blue team.

The results? The experimental referee group awarded significantly more red and yellow cards against the blue team for 'certain' fouls than the control group. Meanwhile, 'certain' fouls made by the opposing team saw the experimental group award significantly fewer cards than the control group.

The decision to focus on teams wearing predominately blue kits is important because this colour is generally linked with feelings of calmness and trust, making it extremely unlikely that the results could be explained by this factor. It has been suggested that the colour of a team's kit might influence the attitude of match officials. Indeed, a study published in the journal '*Psychology of Sport and Exercise*' found that referees judged tackles from behind more harshly for players wearing red than blue.[6] Red being the colour most closely associated with aggressive behaviour.

In a similar vein, another study investigated whether referees were influenced by the relative heights of two players in determining which one should be penalised for fouls.[7] Height representing a good proxy for "dominance and power."

There were three main findings. First, data on fouls awarded by referees from the Bundesliga, UEFA Champions League and FIFA World Cups all showed 'foul perpetrators' were on average taller than their assumed victims. Second, people, when presented with ambiguous foul situations, were more likely to attribute fouls to the taller player. Third, when viewing ambiguous foul situations, participants anticipated the smaller player going to ground more often than their taller opponent. They tended to attribute falls by smaller players to fouls, whereas taller players were considered more likely to be diving in such circumstances.

Put all this together and it seems highly probable that most 50-50s that are adjudged to be fouls and involve two players of noticeably different heights will go the way of the smaller player. This is particularly likely if they fall over in the process.

Nationality bias

Earlier in the book, I referred to the halo effect, whereby people automatically extrapolate an initial positive (or negative) conclusion about one aspect of a person to their whole being. That aspect could be just about anything, including their nationality.

Perhaps we shouldn't be surprised therefore, that a

study of UEFA Champions League (UCL) referees found evidence of an own-nationality bias in their decision-making.[8] While the nationality of match officials for UCL games are never the same as the teams competing, those teams can include players of the same nationality as the officials.

Based on data from 12 seasons of the UCL, the researchers discovered that players from the same country as the match officials benefited to the tune of about 10% when it came to decisions about fouls. A not insignificant advantage, which *increased* to 15-20% if the player was part of the national team, playing at home or featuring in the latter stages of the tournament. Elite referees were found to "exhibit as much, or more, own-nationality bias as their less experienced counterparts."

Given these results and bearing in mind the ease with which judgements are formed and extrapolated, it is not a big leap to imagine that referees will favour teams, players and/or managers they like and penalise those they dislike when making close calls. This is not to say that they are aware of what they are doing — they almost certainly aren't — but to believe that referees' actions, including those at the top level, are free from partisanship would be naive.

For this reason, we *should* take David Coote's remarks about Liverpool and its then-manager seriously. Nobody, including Coote himself, can credibly claim that his words were not reflected in his on-field actions.

VAR to the rescue?

From the range of studies I have cited, it is clear that match officials are not only subject to a variety of unconscious (System 1) biases, but act upon them as well. In other words, they are just like the rest of us. In one way, this is disappointing given that, *unlike* the rest of us, they are presumably made aware of relevant cognitive biases and their effects as part of their training. At the same time, however, it highlights how difficult it is to counteract them.

This brings me to the subject of Video Assistant Referees (VARs). Introduced in the English Premier League in the 2019/20 season, VAR aims to reduce the number of officiating mistakes, allowing for the reversal of original decisions based on video evidence. To what extent does it achieve this aim?

The raw statistics for the 2023/24 season — the latest available — shed light on this:

- 1,300 key decisions were assessed by VAR with an average of 0.29 interventions per game to overturn on-field decisions. That works out to be roughly 1 in every 3.5 games.

- According to the independent Key Match Incident (KMI) Panel, there were 105 correct VAR calls and 31 incorrect ones The latter comprised of incidents when VAR makes an error having intervened, where it intervened when it was inappropriate to do so and where it failed to intervene in a patently incorrect on-field decision.

For the record, the KMI panel has five members made up of three former players and/or coaches as well as one representative from the Premier League and another from Professional Game Match Officials Limited (PGMOL).

Two things strike me about this data. First, VAR interventions to reverse on-field judgements were quite rare. This is largely because its remit is severely restricted.

In the words of the Premier League, it should "only be used for 'clear and obvious errors' or 'serious missed incidents' in four match-changing situations: goals, penalty decisions, direct red card incidents and mistaken identity." The philosophy of VAR is described as "minimum interference – maximum benefit."

Plainly, the League accepts that there are downsides to the use of VAR, not least the disruption it causes to the flow of matches. Indeed, VAR checks delayed games by an average of 60 seconds in the 2023/24 season, triggering plenty of frustration along the way. That frustration in turn prompted the Premier League to issue new guidance at the start of the 2024/25 season, designed to reduce the waiting period. It has worked to a degree, with the average delay down to 40 seconds by early February 2025. Ahead of the new season, Howard Webb, Chief Refereeing Officer for PGMOL, also took the opportunity to emphasise how he wanted VAR to be used:

"We know here that people don't want forensic examination when that's not necessary. We're looking for those clear errors that should jump off the screen and if that doesn't exist in the situation then 'check complete' and we move on."

In short, VAR should intervene (even) less frequently and spend less time doing so. While this is good news for the continuity of games, it is bad news for the accuracy of decision-making.

Second, the ratio of incorrect VAR interventions to correct ones (31/105) was alarmingly high: more than 23% of VAR interventions proving to be wrong according to the KMI panel. Although this had improved to 13/66 (a 17% error rate) after 23 (of 38) rounds of matches in the 2024/25 season, the message is loud and clear: VAR itself is far from infallible. Not a huge surprise. After all, with the possible exception of home-bias, video referees are subject to the same biases as on-field officials.

There is one additional influence — a social one — that is relevant to VAR decisions as well. Off-field officials may want to protect their on-field colleagues. This was illustrated perfectly by Premier League referee Mike Dean in August 2022. Speaking after a controversial match between Chelsea and Tottenham, in which Dean was the VAR, he informed us:

"*I said to* (referee) *Anthony* (Taylor) *afterwards: 'I just didn't want to send you to the screen after what has gone on in the game.' I didn't want to send him up because he is a mate as well as a referee and I think I didn't want to send him up because I didn't want any more grief than he already had.*"

PGMOL subsequently bent over backwards to stress that this was "an isolated incident," but it can't be sure of this. Who knows how prevalent this is?

All in all, VAR undoubtedly reduces the number of 'big' officiating mistakes that are allowed to stand in games. Roughly 100 match-altering errors a season are eliminated in the Premier League. That's the good news. The bad news is that VAR itself is subject to biases and makes errors partly as a result. Also, it is discouraged from intervening when it comes to close calls and is not allowed to step-in when 'smaller' officiating mistakes are made. Of course, those smaller errors could still end up affecting games in significant ways. Think about the awarding of cards. While VAR can intervene in the case of straight red cards, it can't for yellow cards and yet two yellow cards equal a red.

The balance between too many VAR interventions and too few is a difficult one to strike and, to a large extent, boils down to personal preference. Whatever transpires over the long term, however, it is certain that refereeing bias will remain part of the game.

Cricketing biases

If you think football referees are important in influencing outcomes and have a tricky job to do, then consider the role played by cricket umpires, particularly when it comes to LBW (Leg Before Wicket) decisions.

Every time the ball hits the batter and the bowling team appeals, the umpire must decide whether the batter is out. To do so, they are required to predict whether the ball would have gone on to hit the stumps, having previously determined whether it made contact with the batter in line with the stumps (unless the batter wasn't playing a stroke) and the ball didn't pitch outside the line of leg stump! It is not easy, particularly as it only takes about ½ second for the ball to reach the batter and the umpire must (generally) first look at the bowler's feet to determine whether they have overstepped the 'popping crease.' Roughly 15% of all dismissals in cricket come from LBW decisions.

Catches are adjudicated on as well, which is not always as simple as it sounds. Sometimes the batter will get the faintest of 'nicks' on the ball, which may or may not be audible to the umpire standing more than 22 yards away. Other noises might also lead the umpire to think the batter has 'edged' the ball when they haven't. About 17% of dismissals are the result of being caught by the wicketkeeper.

What about stumpings and run outs? Here, umpires must determine whether the batter's foot or bat is over the popping crease when the bails are dislodged, all of which plays out in the blink of an eye. 3% of dismissals are run outs and 2% stumpings.

The fact that umpires have a lot of complex decisions

to make under significant pressure over many hours means mistakes are inevitable. When it comes to LBWs, for example, it is estimated that at least a quarter of on-field decisions are wrong. But what is the evidence that officials are *biased* in their decision-making?

In contrast to football, there is a paucity of studies that address this question. We can gain some insight, however, from research published by Abhinav Sacheti (and colleagues) from Nottingham University in 2015.[9] Using data from 1,000 Test matches between 1986 and 2012, Sacheti tested for the presence of home bias by umpires in their LBW decisions and whether it changed with the introduction of neutral umpires. He discovered a clear bias in favour of the home team when both on-field umpires were of the same nationality as the home team (up to 1994). The bias halved when just one was from the home nation (1994-2002) and all but evaporated when both umpires were neutral (2002-2012). The difference between the first and third periods was equivalent to one less LBW decision in favour of the home team per innings: a big effect.

Given that home advantage is absent when both umpires are from a third country, the implication is that the crowd has little or no bearing on their decisions. This is supported by other analysis in the same research paper and likely reflects the relatively small and more passive nature of fans at most Test matches as well as the introduction of the Decision Review System (DRS) — cricket's equivalent of VAR.

Launched in November 2009, DRS allows teams to check, via a third off-field umpire, whether the on-field decision was correct. Hawk-Eye, infrared and other systems are used to determine the accuracy of the initial judgement with both teams having three (unsuccessful) reviews at their disposal per innings in Test matches.

Unlike VAR, almost all DRS judgements are objective, the result of the technologies used, and don't prove particularly disruptive given the more stop-start nature of cricket. Arguably, the game actually benefits from the extra bit of theatre that results. The system is present for all international matches, but absent from most domestic games.

Since DRS was introduced, an intriguing anti-batter umpiring bias has come to light. Research by Ram Shivakumar revealed that 'out' LBW decisions by on-field umpires were at least 75% more likely to be reversed (to 'not out') by DRS than 'not out' decisions (to 'out').[10] This was based on challenges to umpires' decisions during 126 Test matches between November 2009 and December 2014.

Shivakumar argued that whereas umpires would previously give batters the benefit of the doubt in LBW decisions, the advent of DRS has effectively proved that they were too conservative, leading them to swing (too far) the other way. Contrary to conventional wisdom, however, the proportion of LBWs in total dismissals has not risen in a meaningful way as one would expect if this were true.

A more straightforward explanation is that batters are just better at reviewing LBW decisions than the bowling team. Apart from anything else, they should have a clearer idea whether the ball hit their bat before contacting their pads, in which case they cannot legitimately be given out LBW.

In truth, neither batters nor bowlers have a particularly good record when it comes to reviewing LBW decisions: overall, the success rate is little more than 20% or one in five. In many instances, those choosing to review are doing so in the knowledge that the on-field decision is unlikely to be overturned but the gamble is worth taking.

But I suspect cricketers are also subject to action bias — mentioned in chapter 3 — when it comes to reviews. No doubt it feels better to do something than tamely accept the umpire's decision, particularly when that decision is likely to have significant consequences for the outcome of the match. They don't want to be left regretful.

In brief

It is easy to forget that the vast majority of decisions made by match officials are correct! Most estimates suggest referees and umpires are right around 95% of the time. Nevertheless, in games of small margins, officiating mistakes can make all the difference.

Many argue that this is part of the game and should be accepted as such given the potentially disruptive and dehumanising influence of technology, not to mention its cost. They have a point, but this is a far easier case to present when the errors made are random. Plainly, this is not the case. As we have discovered, some mistakes reflect inherent cognitive biases: a function of the mental shortcuts human beings take to arrive at split-second decisions. Dermot Gallagher's argument that referees lack sufficient time to be prejudiced may be right at a conscious level, but represents a fundamental misunderstanding of unconscious bias.

In football, almost all teams, players and fans believe that match officials are systematically biased against them, which, ironically, is a bias in itself and obviously untrue. Nevertheless, there are plenty of circumstances when they should be wary, even when VAR is available. Referees have been shown to be biased against away teams when it comes to disciplinary actions, stoppage time and penalty kicks. They often penalise underdogs, while generally favouring more successful teams, and, in some circumstances, smaller players and players of the same nationality as themselves. Wearing a predominately red kit may occasionally bring disadvantages as well. In theory, these biases could cancel each other out in any given match, but this is obviously far from guaranteed.

Cricketing biases are not as well researched but appear to include an anti-batter prejudice when it comes to LBW decisions. Action bias helps explain why both batters and bowlers have a poor record when it comes to reviewing on-field umpiring decisions.

7
WINNING AND LOSING

"I hate to lose more than I love to win"

Jimmy Connors, former world number 1 tennis player

We dislike losing as much as we enjoy winning, right? Wrong!

Say somebody offered you a chance of winning or losing £1,000 on the toss of an unbiased coin. Would you take the bet? If you are like most people, you would turn down the opportunity. What about if they offered £1,100 for a correct call and a £1,000 loss if you got it wrong? Again, most would decline. How about £1,500 v £1,000? Psychologists have discovered that it normally requires a potential gain of 1.5 to 2.5 times the potential loss for people to accept a bet of this nature. Jimmy Connors is not alone in hating losing more than he enjoys winning. We are all instinctively Loss Averse.

This psychological peculiarity of ours is generally considered to have an evolutionary origin — our chances of survival were improved by prioritising threats over opportunities — and carries many practical implications today, not least in sport. When competing against another person or team, System 1 tells us that it would be better to strive to avoid a loss than to seek a win. This may seem like a minor difference but involves a completely different mindset — one where we are reluctant to take risks, preferring to play it safe, to defend rather than attack. Only when losing do we instinctively become risk-seeking, particularly if there is not much time left to retrieve the situation.

Let's look at how this pans out in the context of three sports: golf, football and cricket.

Golf

One of the best known examples of loss aversion in sport involves the comparative success of par and birdie (one under par) putts. The theory is that the fear of *losing* a stroke (relative to par) leads players to concentrate more and hit the ball harder, giving the ball a better chance of reaching the hole, than they do when attempting to *gain* a stroke relative to par.

A study published in the American Economic Review put this to the test.[1] Based on a massive dataset of more than 1.6 million putts attempted by 188 professional golfers in 204 PGA tournaments between 2004 and 2008, the authors concluded:

"*for a given distance, golfers are approximately 2-4 percentage points more likely to make pars than they are to make birdie putts.*"

Although the very best golfers were found to be less prone to this effect, every single player, including Tiger Woods, exhibited some degree of loss aversion.

The extent of the 'accuracy gap' was found to diminish

as tournaments progressed. Whereas par putts were 4% more likely to be made than birdies in Round 1, the difference fell to 2.1% in Round 4. It was argued that referencing to par is more relevant at the start of tournaments than the end, when an alternative reference point – what other golfers are scoring – becomes more pertinent. Par is not necessarily the reference point for most amateur golfers. Their benchmark maybe one over par, in which case they are likely to be slightly more successful when putting for that score than for par itself.

The study also found that professional golfers hit birdie and eagle putts significantly softer than they did par, bogey and double bogey putts, partly explaining the lower success rate of the former than the latter. Although softer putts that missed the hole generally brought the advantage of making the subsequent putt easier, the study discovered that players would have been better served by fully committing to the birdie/eagle putt in the first place. In effect, to treat it as if they were putting for par. If they had, their scoring would have been lower and their prize money correspondingly higher. But despite the huge incentive to change, it is doubtful that many players have successfully taken on board this lesson. The problem being that it feels wrong. Their intuition and instinct are always urging them to do the opposite.

Football

Consider the following: if the scores are level in a football match, a team potentially *gains* two points by scoring a goal, while they are at risk of *losing* two points if they concede a goal when winning one-nil. With two points at stake in both situations, one might expect effort levels to be the same as well. But this would be to assume that football players are not subject to loss aversion. Loss aversion tells us that losing two points is psychologically more painful than gaining two points, meaning players are likely to exert more effort in the second situation than the first.

Current match situation	**Points gained by scoring one goal***	**Points lost by conceding one goal***
Winning by two or more goals	0	0
Winning by one goal	0	**2**
Drawing	**2**	1
Losing by one goal	1	0
Losing by two or more goals	0	0

* Assuming the score then remains unchanged for the rest of the match

A German study set out to investigate the presence of loss aversion based on data from three seasons of the Bundesliga (2011/12, 2012/13 and 2013/14), totalling 918 matches.[2] Effort levels were proxied by players' running distance per minute on the pitch as well as their number of sprints and high intensity runs, again on a per minute basis. Of all score lines, it found that players exerted the greatest effort when their team was leading by a single goal. In other words, when they had the most to lose from conceding a goal, *not* when they had the most to gain from scoring a goal. Specifically:

"*Relative to a tied score, a player runs approximately 3.5 meters more per minute and provides one additional intensive run every three minutes when leading by one goal.*"

When trailing by a single goal, players expended significantly *less* energy than they did when the scores were level. This again supports the presence of loss aversion. While a team (potentially) gains one point by scoring when it is one-nil down, it may lose one point by conceding in a draw situation. The latter looms larger in the minds of most players, encouraging them to work harder.

The authors considered a host of alternative explanations for these phenomena, including relative team quality and the differing nature of substitutions depending on the score line at the time, but none affected the results in a meaningful way.

Another research paper investigated the risk appetite of teams in different game states.[3] Risk-taking was represented by a team's attacking intensity which in turn was measured by the number of shots on and off target, blocked shots, free kicks and corner kicks. The study used three million events from 1,826 matches played during the 2017-18 season in the top five European football leagues: the English Premier League, Spanish La Liga, Italian Serie A, German Bundesliga and French Ligue 1.

It revealed that attack intensity was higher for losing teams and lower for leading teams compared with those match situations when scores were level. This conclusion — risk-taking in the realms of potential losses and risk aversion in the realms of potential gains — is consistent with loss aversion and seems entirely sensible…until one realises that the risks taken by losing teams often backfire. According to the study, teams in the lead had more shots on target than those that were losing or drawing, while the latter had more shots off target, blocked shots and corner kicks. In other words, teams become more attack minded when they are losing, but the attacks themselves become less effective. Shots are taken before it is sensible to do so, for example.

It was argued that the results "may support the negative relationship between performance and risk-taking, which is stronger for losing teams than for winning teams" found by other researchers. This is an extremely important conclusion, running counter to the way teams, players and managers often behave. To clarify, it doesn't mean that it is always bad to take risks, but rather that those risks should be calculated–clear-headed, not panicky. As we will see in the next section, this is not an easy balance to strike.

The broader implication of these results is that league topping teams are likely to play more defensively than they would otherwise do, particularly if their league position runs counter to expectations, while teams in the relegation zone will take greater risks. Neither approach is necessarily the most suitable. The problem with the former is that it probably involves moving away from methods that have got them to where they are and, in the case of the latter, excessive risk-taking is unlikely to yield benefits other than perhaps to appease supporters and owners. Relegation threatened teams are probably much better served attempting to improve the quality of their existing players through training, trying to bring in new players with greater ability and/or their adjusting tactics in sensible ways.

Players and managers are not the only ones subject to loss aversion in football. So are supporters. Several studies have found that crowds are larger when the home team is likely to win or are huge underdogs as opposed to games where the outcome is highly uncertain.[4] The same is also true of TV audiences and runs counter to conventional wisdom that suggests potential viewers are more interested in games considered likely to be closely fought.[5]

Cricket

While I am unaware of any rigorous statistical studies of loss aversion in cricket, there is no shortage of anecdotal evidence that supports the notion, particularly when it comes to the shorter forms of the game. We see batting teams take undue risks when they begin highly challenging run chases, frequently imploding as a result, while they often do the opposite when confronting a low score, ensuring the match is closer than it should be.

The sport also provides evidence of what happens when a team actively attempts to eliminate loss aversion. It stems from the England Test cricket team's startling performances following the appointment of Ben Stokes as captain and Brendon McCullum as head coach in May 2022–a case study of huge psychological and sporting interest.

Chris Stocks, cricket journalist at *The I* newspaper, identified seven principles that underpin the pair's unique approach to Test cricket, widely known as 'Bazball' (Baz being McCullum's nickname):

- A less reflective environment
- No negative chat
- A win-at-all-costs mentality
- No fear of failure
- Praise – even for little things
- Simplicity of message
- Embracing mental freedom and fun

The primary aim is to take pressure off the players, allowing them to express themselves without fear of the consequences. Mistakes aren't punished or overanalysed. Instead, positive, risk-embracing cricket is rewarded, partly through consistency of selection.

The following is how Stokes himself has explained the benefits of Bazball, particularly as it relates to batting:

"*When you take that burden off individuals and the team, you see players excelling and showing more within themselves. No one is worried about getting out. You don't want to get out…but when that fear of failure isn't there, you're not tentative and you make better decisions.*" (December 2022)

"*The message was run into the fear of what the game was rather than stand still or back away from it. I'll say it quite simply, we were either winning this game or losing it. That was the mentality we wanted all the batters coming in to have…When you have the backing of the coach and myself saying what I say about how we want to go about things, it obviously rubs off on the players in a very, very positive way, so you're not fearing failure. If anything, you're just going out and doing what you want to do.*" (June 2022)

As for Stokes' methods in the field — those times when England are bowling — McCullum said:

"*He seems to have taken captaincy to a new level…What we see on the field pulling the strings…he's constantly active, making plays and always thinking about wickets and he's so consistent with his message that he doesn't care about runs…his general positivity is quite staggering.*" (December 2022)

The leadership team has radically altered the metrics by which players are selected for England as well. Rather than relying almost exclusively on past performances in red ball cricket at county level, the character of players, their point(s) of difference and the potential they offer have all gained much greater prominence. Several players have been picked despite featuring in just a handful of first-class games and not necessarily successfully so.

It is in these ways that Stokes and McCullum have, in

effect, shifted the team's loss aversion ratio — the weight given to potential losses relative to potential gains. While, as we saw earlier, the psychological pain for most people of losing is about 1.5-2 times more than the enjoyment of winning, it is much closer to 1 — possibly below it — amongst the England Test team. As such, the players have become the sporting equivalent of financial market traders, perfectly willing to risk losing in the belief that this improves their chances of winning.

The most tangible indication of the change in mindset has been the jump in the speed with which runs are scored by England's batters. While the team registered an average run rate of 3.1 per over between January 2020 and April 2022, closely aligned to the other Test playing nations at the time, it has jumped to an astonishing 4.6 since then. This is one run per over — or 90 runs in a typical day of Test match cricket — above that of any other country in the same period. It is also unmatched in the history of the game with Steve Waugh's Australian teams of 1999-2004 the closest at 3.7.

The initial turnaround in results was equally staggering: following a sequence of one win in seventeen prior to Bazball, Stokes won ten of his first eleven matches as captain with largely unchanged personnel. Subsequently, however, results have been far patchier. In the last twenty games to April 2025 (before the start of the English summer), he has triumphed nine times, lost ten times and drawn once when the weather intervened on the final day to prevent a result.

Looking at Stokes' overall record, excluding the single match he captained before landing the job on a permanent basis, his win rate is still a highly impressive 61.3%, better than any of the other twenty-three England captains that have led the side more than fifteen times. At the same time, however, his loss rate of 35.5% compares unfavourably with most others. Only 6 of the twenty-three have an inferior record.

The best way of making sense of this is to compare Stokes' win/loss ratio (1.7) with those of his predecessors. Eight of the twenty-three enjoyed a higher ratio, with Mike Brearley and Percy Chapman equal top at 4.5, while, in more recent times, both Michael Vaughan (2.4) and Andrew Strauss (2.2) have outperformed Stokes. Such comparisons don't take account of the underlying strength of the teams captained by these players relative to those of their opponents, but there is nothing to suggest that Stokes has an historically poor group of players at his disposal or the competition is any tougher. In fact, it is probably easier to make the opposite argument.

At this stage of the Bazball experiment, two things are clear. First, draws are effectively a thing of the past, an anathema to Stokes. This makes him very unusual. Former South African captain, Faf du Plessis, is the only other Test match captain that has a draw percentage of less than 10%. Second, the margins by which the team are winning or losing matches are often unusually large. With significant risk-taking has come, not surprisingly, significant volatility in performances.

It is far less obvious that Bazball represents a pathway to sustained success. A cynic might even suggest that the many triumphs of the first 18 months of the McCullum/Stokes era reflected little more than a 'new manager bounce.'

Whether Stokes can ultimately replicate the success of England's premier captains (in terms of wins versus loses) depends heavily on whether the team can improve its risk management. It must get better at recognising those times when it is wiser to defend than to attack — to absorb pressure rather than to exert it — and playing aggressive (not reckless) cricket when exerting pressure on the opposition.

These are fine lines to tread and ones which the team has, so far, frequently fallen the wrong side of, particularly when batting against spin. The players often seem to take the view that sooner or later there will be "a ball with my name on it" (an unplayable delivery that will get them out) meaning that they should try and make the most runs in the shortest possible time. It is a surprisingly negative opinion for a team so dedicated to positivity. Wouldn't it be better to practise harder and longer against high-quality spin bowling instead?

I suspect the simplicity of messaging, so fundamental to Bazball, gets in the way of a more nuanced approach as well. Stokes himself sometimes bats in an exaggerated way that appears to be sending a very deliberate message to his teammates. The trouble is they don't always appear to cotton on or, perhaps, lack the technical skill to replicate his approach.

It has been a very deliberate ploy to take the England team to the opposite end of the risk-taking spectrum to the one normally occupied by Test cricketers. We have seen the results and the question now is will the approach be refined? Are Stokes and McCullum willing to dial-down the degree of risk-taking at times and, if so, can the players successfully adapt? It is not going to be easy.

In brief

As human beings, we hate losing more than we enjoy winning, meaning we are naturally inclined to shirk risk when ahead and embrace risk when behind. The sporting consequences can be profound.

A professional golfer is more likely to be successful when putting for par than for birdie. Although the consequence of missing both putts is the same – one additional stroke being added to their score – they inherently dislike losing a stroke relative to par more than they enjoy gaining a stroke. Consequently, they focus more intently and hit the ball harder when it comes to the former than the latter.

Meanwhile, footballers have been found to run further and sprint more frequently when they are winning 1-0 than when scores are level. The thought of drawing when they are in a winning position represents a more potent source of motivation than the thought of winning when they are drawing, even though two points are at stake in both cases.

Not surprisingly, a team that goes behind in a game becomes more attack-minded, taking greater risks as it attempts to regain parity. The thing is, not only does this leave it more vulnerable at the back, but the attacks themselves have been shown to become less effective: shooting when it would be better to pass or crossing from deeper positions than they otherwise would. Put another way, losing teams and their managers often act in ways that *increase* their chances of losing.

Brendon McCullum and Ben Stokes have embraced risk to a degree never seen before in Test match cricket and not just when England are losing. The results have been extraordinary. Draws are a thing of the past, while the cricket played is more action-packed, piquing interest in a format of the game that is under existential pressure. Whether Bazball has improved England's win/loss ratio, beyond an initial bounce, is more debatable, however. Breathtaking victories have been combined with devastating losses suggesting that reducing loss aversion is not without its perils. The main difficulty comes in judging the appropriate degree of risk to take in each situation before executing the necessary skills successfully. It is something that the team has conspicuously failed to achieve on occasion and, I suspect, will continue to struggle with.

8
CROWDS AND FANDOM

"Such is the nature of crowds: either they are humble and servile or arrogant and dominating. They are incapable of making moderate use of freedom, which is the middle course, or of keeping it"

Titus Livius, Roman historian (died 17AD)

Sporting occasions feel very different when fans are absent. If we didn't know this before COVID struck, then we most certainly do now. How strange it was watching 'big' matches while being able to hear the individual voices of the players and coaching staff. Clearly, crowds provide atmosphere, adding meaning to matches, while, as we saw earlier, they also influence outcomes.

They do something else as well: change the behaviour of spectators, sometimes radically. Otherwise quiet, empathetic people can become loud and aggressive when part of a crowd, ranting at those deemed to be getting in the way of their team's success or enjoying the emotional pain felt by opposition supporters whose team is losing. You may even have found yourself saying or doing things you wouldn't normally dream of saying or doing.

The psychological grip crowds hold over the individual fans they are composed of is extraordinary and something I will investigate in this chapter, along with the fascinating subject of fandom itself. Why is it, for example, that we pay a lot of money — money we can ill afford sometimes — to watch people we have never met play a game? Why do we fall in love with a particular team and remain loyal to it even when it is performing poorly?

Crowds

In the late-1960s, an American psychologist by the name of Philip Zimbardo undertook an unusual experiment involving several willing participants.[1] Some were asked to wear hoods and cloaks that hid their identity, while others wore normal clothes and name tags. Both groups were then asked one by one to administer electric shocks to another individual every time that person made a mistake while attempting to learn something. For the record, the shocks were fake, although this was (initially) unbeknown to those inflicting them. The study discovered that those masking their identity administered significantly longer shocks relative to the plain-clothes group, suggesting that anonymity promoted higher levels of aggression.

What has this got to do with crowds? In similar fashion to disguises, being part of a crowd makes us feel more anonymous and less accountable for our actions. To coin the technical term, they 'de-individualise' us, potentially explaining why our behaviour changes when surrounded by large numbers of other people.

According to both Gustave Le Bon, who wrote a highly influential book on crowd psychology back in 1895,[2] and the infamous psychologist Sigmund Freud, the nature of our behaviour in crowd situations is likely to be primitive and hedonistic. Freud postulated that becoming a member of a crowd serves to unlock the unconscious mind, meaning we act on antisocial impulses that we would otherwise curb. Primal instincts effectively take charge as the restraining effects of individual morality and social conditioning are temporarily washed away. If this sounds about right, then it is probably because the mental image we have of crowds is often of a baying mob shouting obscenities.

In truth, however, people's behaviour doesn't always descend to the lowest common denominator in crowd situations. Take crowds at rugby games, for example. Here, fans of opposing teams sit happily together and are generally highly respectful of both sides. At Lord's cricket ground in London, nicknamed the Home of Cricket, the overwhelming noise is a contented hum interspersed with the odd ripple of applause and occasional roar of approval.

Alcohol is consumed, often in significant quantities, at cricket matches and while this can lead to increasingly raucous behaviour as the day wears on, crowds rarely become belligerent. If anger does materialise it is usually directed at officials putting a stop to rapidly growing 'beer snakes' or removing inflatable balls that have found their way onto the outfield. Even in football, supporters are typically well-mannered when injured players of either team are stretchered from the pitch or a minute's silence/applause is held to remember former players that have recently died. There is plenty of supportive chanting and singing at football matches as well.

To make sense of the range of behaviours displayed by sporting crowds we must understand the role played by social norms; those unwritten behavioural codes I referred to in chapter 3. Not only are they very powerful in dictating the behaviour of individuals within crowds but their nature varies enormously across different sports, venues, countries and circumstances. Clearly, it is not the done thing to turn up at Lords and abuse opposition players, for example. If people do, they are quickly expelled or suspended as three MCC members discovered to their cost during an Ashes Test match in July 2023. The story is very different when it comes to football matches. Here, expletives directed at match officials, managers, opposition supporters and players have been normalised in crowd situations.

Contrasting norms explain why the same person can attend a game of cricket and a football match and yet behave in very different ways.

So how does this observation fit with the results of Zimbardo's experiment? It may be that those dressed in cloaks and hoods behaved more vindictively than those wearing everyday clothes, *not* because they were anonymised but because they associated hooded disguises with errant actions. The provision of lengthy electric shocks was the behaviour they thought was expected of them given what they were wearing. A later study supported this explanation as participants who dressed in Ku Klux Klan robes shocked a research collaborator far more than those dressed as nurses, regardless of whether they were identifiable or not.[3]

The more difficult question to address is who or what dictates the specific norms that operate within crowds?

Convergence Theory postulates that crowd behaviour is not a product of the crowd itself but rather the crowd is a product of the coming together of like-minded individuals. According to this hypothesis, the individuals that make up crowds behave in the same way as they would alone, only more so. While there is doubtless some truth to this, it doesn't explain why the same person's behaviour can change so radically depending on the sport they are watching.

Some have argued that the contrasting nature of sports is a factor–football being a shorter, more intense game than cricket, involving plenty of physical contact. It is suggested that this translates into a more emotionally charged atmosphere both on the pitch and in the stands and hence higher levels of aggression. The obvious counter to this is that rugby is far more physical than football and can be equally intense. Yet, rugby crowds are generally much better behaved than their footballing equivalents.

What about how the players themselves behave? Do crowds take their lead from them? Famously, it has been said that "Football is a gentlemen's game played by hooligans and rugby is a hooligan's game played by gentlemen." But while rugby players are usually far more respectful of referees than their footballing equivalents, fights between players regularly break out in full view of the crowd, often going unpunished by the officials. The same is not true of football.

Fans' behaviour can be heavily influenced by a few select individuals or 'crowd leaders.' There are limits, however. It seems unlikely that even the most charismatic of individuals could persuade a group of typical football supporters to welcome opposition fans into their area of the stadium or sing inoffensive, mildly humorous songs about their opponents! The leaders are almost always representative of the fans or 'ultras' they control, otherwise they would lack the credibility necessary to lead.

To my mind, the most convincing answer relates to the influence stereotyping (a System 1 function) has on social norms. Ask a representative sample of people for three words they associate with football crowds and I suspect hostility (or words of similar meaning) would feature regularly. The stereotypical football crowd is *not* one where everybody looks cherubic and behaves beautifully.

The stereotype will deter many people from attending matches, while those going will do so in anticipation of a degree of antagonistic behaviour. Most will be willing to participate in it as well, partly because this is what is deemed necessary to fit in. And if enough people hold the same view, then antagonistic behaviour will reveal itself, particularly if it is encouraged by crowd-leaders.

Ask the same sample of people about cricket or rugby crowds and their answers are likely to be very different. Again, those that choose to attend a match will expect behaviours in line with the stereotype they hold and which they are happy to replicate. In short, the stereotypes set the social norms and become self-fulfilling as a result.

A detailed assessment of how the stereotypes themselves developed is beyond the scope of this chapter, but a couple of observations are worth making.

It is interesting that the crowds at women's professional football matches behave very differently from those at their male equivalents. To quote comments from a recent reddit thread on the subject:

"There's always been a family feel...to WSL (Women's Super League) games and I love that because I've always felt more comfortable at women's than at men's games."

"All the time I've been, I've only ever seen people be respectful of each other."

"The game at Wembley was mixed in the area we were sat in and it was a really nice atmosphere. It's the opposite to men's football, everyone is there to enjoy the match and watch the game."

The fanbase is very different from the men's game, helping explain the different stereotypes and social norms associated with the women's game. Now these norms are established they are likely to prove highly resistant to change for the same reasons that tribal behaviour has become entrenched in professional men's matches.

This is not to say, however, that norms are always and everywhere set in stone. According to Kick It Out, the anti-discrimination organisation, reports of homophobic mass chanting fell from 43 in the 2022/23 English season to 17 in 2023/24. It put the improvement down to a "a change in the law and updated FA guidance where certain chants have become a chargeable offence." Sadly, these are the sort of measures required to force adjustments in behaviour and even then they may not be sufficient.

The same organisation reported a 47% rise (496 to 731) in racist abuse across all levels of the game in 2023/24 compared with the previous season, while faith-based discriminatory reports were up 34%. These increases came even though it is illegal to incite racial hatred or verbally abuse anybody because of their race. In these instances, the anonymity offered by crowd situations is relevant. Although technology is making it easier to identify perpetrators, male football, in particular, still has a long way to go to stamp out unacceptable behaviours.

Fandom

You won't be surprised to know that psychology plays a large part in explaining our peculiar obsessions with sporting teams. Let's start with why we support them in the first place.

Referencing multiple studies across different levels of competition, Professor Daniel Wann at Murray State University in the US, an expert in sports psychology, pointed out:

"*the more the fan is identified with a team, the greater that individual is likely to have a well-rounded sense of psychological health, lower levels of loneliness, lower levels of alienation, a higher sense of self-esteem and less social isolation.*"[4]

The suggestion is that being a fan benefits our mental well-being. But why should be the case?

It is widely accepted that good mental health is dependent on meeting several basic psychological needs. These include feeling a sense of belonging, experiencing frequent social contact, knowing that there is meaning to what we do and having a degree of structure to our lives. Closely identifying ourselves with a sporting team or individual can help satisfy these psychological cravings, particularly if we go to the trouble of attending games in person.

In this context, it is interesting to observe how easily we slip into using the words 'us,' 'our' and 'we' when talking about the team we support, signifying that sense of belonging, while reinforcing it at the same time. We do so even though we have no way of influencing the team's performance as an individual fan.

One thing we *can't* say about being a sports fan is that it brings endless satisfaction and joy. A fascinating study published by the National Institute of Economic and Social Research (NIESR) in 2018 set out to discover how people's happiness was affected by their football team's outcomes.[5] The results, shown on the next page, were based on data from three million responses submitted by 32,000 individuals via an app. They show how happiness scores changed within the first hour of their team's result.

Not surprisingly, winning provided a mood boost and losing the opposite, the effects being felt more intensely when the individual was physically present at the match. The more interesting points were that draws were met with discontent, while fans were negatively impacted by defeats to a greater extent than they were positively affected by victories. The unhappiness triggered by a loss also lasted longer than the positivity generated by a win, meaning the aggregate impact of defeats was found to be up to *four times* larger than that of victories. That's quite a lot of unhappiness!

Match Result and Location	**Impact on Happiness Score**
Win, respondent didn't attend match	+2.4
Win, respondent attended match	+9.8
Draw, respondent didn't attend match	-3.2
Draw, respondent attended match	-3.1
Loss, respondent didn't attend match	-7.2
Loss, respondent attended match	-14.0

Bearing in mind the topic of the previous chapter — loss aversion — we shouldn't be overly surprised by this, although it does beg the question why on earth do we continue supporting a team that loses the majority of its matches?

Maybe we become immune to defeats. If we expect our team to lose and we are right, then perhaps it doesn't hurt that much, whereas an unexpected win is reason for huge cheer. The same study investigated this reasoning, recording the impact on happiness of wins, draws and losses that were anticipated as well as those that weren't.

The penultimate row of the table overleaf shows how happiness was affected within the first hour when a win was not anticipated. Evidently, it still took a meaningful hit. A hit similar to the boost provided an *unanticipated* triumph and twice as large as the benefit provided by a win that was expected.

Match Result and Expectation	Impact on Happiness Score
Win, win not expected	+7.0
Win, win expected	+3.1
Draw, win not expected	-1.9
Draw, win expected	-4.1
Loss, win not expected	-6.3
Loss, win expected	-10.0

Writing in *Psychology Today*, Nir Eyal provided two alternative explanations for fan loyalty in the context of regular defeats: hope and variable rewards.[6] Although we might expect our team to lose, there is always the possibility that it will surprise us, keeping us interested. Thanks to the possibility effect, described in chapter 4, we consistently overestimate that chance. Sure, losses deflate our spirit, but it is not long before we are looking forward to the next game or indeed the next season, with at least a modicum of hope.

As for the effect of variable rewards, Eyal likened our situation as fans to playing slot machines and video games:

"*Random reinforcement kicks the brain's dopamine system into higher gear. We're mesmerised by the prospect of another chance to find a reward, a win, a prize – (it's) an endless search for satisfaction that is never fully satisfied.*"

This makes supporting a team sound like an addiction and indeed, for many, that is exactly what it is. As the NIESR report explained:

"*the addicted person is always trying to get back to the first high. In the football context, this could mean that a football fan selectively remembers the high of the great result in the past and continues following the team, or attending the match, in the hope that this will be repeated.*"

Social factors also play a role in explaining the faithfulness of most fans. As mentioned in chapter 3, fans don't want to be perceived as disloyal to their team. After all, fickleness or glory hunting are generally considered to be signs of weakness. Many friendships originate or flourish as a result of supporting the same team, while dissing the local rival represents a good way to bond as well. Changing team allegiance might just mean changing friends and/or families as well.

My final point relates to the Sunk Cost Fallacy and how it encourages us to stick with a team. Say you bought an Arsenal season ticket at a cost of more than £1,000 at the start of the 2024/25 season (yes, it really was that much), you would probably feel compelled to attend most home matches, even if you weren't enjoying their style of play. Alternatively, you might have decided to spend £140 on Manchester United's 2024/25 "long sleeve home authentic" shirt. Again, you are more likely to keep supporting the club than if you had chosen not to purchase the shirt in the first place.

In these and similar circumstances, we effectively choose to impose a penalty on ourselves for making what has turned out to be a poor decision. We do so because, not unreasonably, we expect to receive a return on our investment and it feels wasteful to give up on it. The bigger the investment, the more reluctant we are to throw in the towel. Take a fan who has supported the same team for thirty years. They are likely to have expended a huge amount of emotion and a vast amount of time and money in doing so. As such, if we were to ask them whether they are thinking of giving up on their team after a lengthy run of poor form and ensuing unhappiness, the answer will almost certainly be "no."

Another trait classically associated with fandom is believing that we know better than the owner or manager! Put in their position, we would undoubtedly do a far superior job.

While this may be correct in a handful of cases, the interesting thing is that most of us are convinced that we belong to that handful of people–a non sequitur. Psychologists label this peculiarity as Illusory Superiority or the Dunning-Kruger effect. It usually occurs in relation to activities deemed to be relatively straightforward and where success is difficult or unlikely to be measured.

Our perceived ability behind the wheel of a car is a great non-sporting example. Here, surveys consistently find that 80-90% of people believe that they are better than average drivers. In fact, a US study discovered that even when using their phone to message or email, a remarkable 80% of people still considered themselves to be an "average" or "above average" driver. I suspect that running a club or managing a team represents another example, although here it is not just a case of believing that we are better than average, but superior to those actually employed to do these things.

Often, it seems obvious that the owner should be improving the club's facilities or the manager should be changing the team in certain ways, and yet they don't, or not sufficiently quickly anyway. Another interesting thing then typically occurs. We quickly conclude that the owner or manager must be stupid or words to that effect. The chances are, however, that we are the ones being a bit dim. Little do we know it, but we are probably committing a Fundamental Attribution Error. Let me explain, again in the context of driving first.

It is interesting to observe that when *we* make a mistake

it is almost always the fault of our situation — a passenger was distracting us, our line of vision was obstructed or there was something wrong with the car — whereas when *others* err it reflects their carelessness, ability or who they are. Apart from our natural inclination to shift blame, the difference in approach is the result of having more information about our own situation than that of our fellow road users. Because we are ignorant of the factor(s) that cause another driver to miscalculate, we look for the easy answer instead – "they're stupid." In sporting situations, the owner or manager may have very good reasons for their actions or lack thereof, we just don't know what they are. On the other hand, of course, they may not!

In brief

The transformative power of crowds on the behaviour of individuals is remarkable and extend beyond the anonymity that such situations offer. It is not as though all people at all sporting events become belligerent when part of a crowd. Indeed, the same person can act very differently depending on the sport they are watching and the specific circumstances involved.

All sports and many situations therein bring with them social norms which dictate individual behaviour within the crowd. It is my contention that these social norms have little to do with the nature of the game itself or the way the players conduct themselves, but stem from stereotyping. People turn up to football matches expecting certain behaviours and go to cricket matches in anticipation of a different type of conduct. They then (generally) act accordingly. Expectations become self-fulfilling in another way as well. Once sporting crowds have gained particular behavioural reputations, they attract more people who act in these ways.

One of the main reasons we are so easily sucked into supporting a team or individual is the many psychological benefits it provides. As well as boosting social contact and gaining a sense of belonging, fandom supplies meaning and structure to our lives. However, as all fans know, identifying with a club also brings disappointment and plenty of it in some cases. A combination of hope, addiction and sunk costs, added to the psychological benefits described, ensure most remain loyal when times are tough.

As fans we love to pass judgement on our own team and competitors. We do so in the unshakeable belief that we know better than the owner, manager and players, many of whom are "just dumb." In most (but not all) instances, this represents Illusory Superiority.

9
FINAL THOUGHTS

"It's a funny old game"

Jimmy Greaves, former Tottenham and England footballer

I began the book by stating that the playing and watching of sport is rife with psychological peculiarities, subsequently exploring the reasons behind these oddities, the implications thereof and, where appropriate, what we can do to overcome them. I have looked at the way in which we think about luck; the strange decisions and judgements we come to; why we can't help making predictions and yet are so poor at them; the oddities of sporting form; the numerous ways in which match officials are biased; the repercussions of players' preference not to lose rather than to win; the behaviour of crowds and our strong attachment to sporting teams.

Instinctive — System 1 — thoughts and the many biases they give rise to are usually responsible for our sporting (and other) idiosyncrasies:

- The brain automatically works to protect our self-esteem: when we have won, it is down to skill and when we have lost, something outside our control, such as bad luck, is typically responsible. Either way, we fail to learn potentially valuable lessons, ones that could bring improvement and future success.

- We distrust coincidences and are suckers for causal stories. It is why weird superstitions, such as the wearing of lucky pants, are so widespread and why pundits earn a living.

- We look for shortcuts and make big assumptions, most of which are extremely helpful but some of which lead to poor choices and naive predictions. We let our emotions rule the roost, make lazy comparisons, stereotype, rely too heavily on previous outcomes, assume that 'what we see is all there is' and so on. No wonder that our record when it comes to sports betting is patchy at best.

- Our memory also plays tricks on us. We are far more likely to recollect significant highs and lows and other extraordinary sporting moments as opposed to the humdrum of events. The result is that we believe the former happen far more regularly than is really the case.

- The vagaries of sporting form often reflect what is going on inside our head. Different sporting situations are associated with different mental schemas which can vary enormously between individuals. Such schemas help determine our levels of anxiety, motivation, resilience and confidence, all of which are key to performance levels.

- Strange, seemingly biased, decisions by match officials are exactly that. As human beings, they are subject to the same sort of thoughts and biases as the rest of us, which they also have a nasty habit of acting on.

- Our brain favours a safety-first approach when we are drawing or winning and the opposite when we are losing. Our tendency is to sit on a lead, taking too few risks, when we should be looking to extend it or alternatively to panic, taking undue risks, when the opposition go in front.

- We are great respecters of learnt social norms. Those norms help explain why sometimes we behave differently in crowd situations and why we are reluctant to change our mind even when the facts suggest we should.

- Fandom offers many psychological advantages but some downsides as well, particularly when our team loses. We dislike losses more than we enjoy wins. Continuing to support a team that loses frequently may reflect the influence of sunk costs or even be a form of addiction.

- The unintended consequences of System 1 thinking are clearly many and various, which is where System 2 potentially comes in. Through

> conscious thought, we can carefully scrutinise our instinctive conclusions, *possibly* coming up with better answers as a result. The problem is, it is time-consuming and effortful to engage System 2, making it a positive hindrance in some sporting situations, while ensuring we are inherently reluctant to use it on those occasions when it might be beneficial.

Most of the time this doesn't cause meaningful difficulties. Occasionally, however, particularly when money or personal well-being is involved, it is wise to try and pause before acting. Ironically, this is most relevant when the solution springs immediately to mind and the way forward seems obvious. In these circumstances, System 1 is highly likely to have provided the answer. We won't eliminate costly mistakes by pondering more and relying on instinctive answers less, but we will reduce our chances of making them.

The following are areas where biases lead us (or others) to do things that *lower* the probability of success and where improvement is possible. All of the 15 suggestions I make below run counter to conventional wisdom or what is usually assumed/done.

- Win, lose or draw, those actively involved in sport should *always* take the opportunity to learn and improve. We should ask ourselves, "what can I do better?"

- Teams should neither sit on a narrow lead, nor take huge risks when losing.

- It *can* be beneficial to change a winning team and leave a losing one intact.

- When playing sport, it is not enough just to anticipate success, we should expect to be lucky as well. Research suggests this brings further psychological and hence performance benefits.

- Be aware that inaction is sometimes better than action.

- *Don't* expect match officials to be fair. Use perceived injustices as reasons to work harder.

- When required to accurately evaluate a player/team, *never* rely solely on a highlights package or how they perform against inferior opposition. Let the data do the talking.

- Assume your memory of events is wrong, unless proven otherwise.

- Pundits are no better and often worse than most of us when it comes to predicting the future, while gut feelings are no guarantee of forecasting success either. Don't rely on them.

- Explanations for sporting success and failure are almost always vastly oversimplified and frequently wrong. Don't trust them.

- Past success/failure, even in very recent times, is not a guarantee of future success/failure. Look back when forecasting the future, but bear in mind history rarely repeats itself exactly.

- Think very carefully before betting on a team or player you support or against ones you dislike.

- Be aware of the tendency to overpredict the probability of unlikely but possible events and underpredict the chances of likely but not certain events.

- Beyond a certain (basic) point, betting doesn't get easier with experience.

- If the facts change, don't be reluctant to change views.

Whether you agree with these suggestions or not, one thing is for sure: it is *always* worth sitting and watching sporting spectacles or participating in sport if you can. After all, you never know what strange things you will witness, not to mention what fortune your lucky pants might bring!

REFERENCES

Introduction

[1] Prior-Wandesforde, R. (2023). *Fallibilities & Peculiarities: Exploring the Odd Things We Think & Do.* UK: Kindle Direct Publishing.

Chapter 1 – Why so curious?

[1] Kahneman, D. (2012). *Thinking, Fast and Slow.* London, UK: Penguin Group.

Chapter 2 – Luck & Destiny

[1] Taleb, N. (2005). *Fooled by Randomness.* New York, NY: Random House.

[2] Mukherjee, A., & Shaikh, A.S. (2022). Superstitious ritual behaviour in sports: A Comparative Study among Various Athletes. *Journal of Sports Research 9*(1), 36-48. https://doi.org/10.18488/90.v9i1.2912.

[3] Martin del Campo Ríos, J., Fuggetta. et al. (2015). Beliefs in being unlucky and deficits in executive functioning: an ERP study. PeerJ 3:e1007. https://doi.org/10.7717/peerj.1007.

[4] Banerjee, K., & Bloom, P. (2014). Why did this happen to me? Religious believers' and non-believers' teleological reasoning about life events. *Cognition, 133*(1), 277-303. https://doi.org/10.1016/j.cognition.2014.06.017.

Chapter 3 – Judgements & Decisions

[1] Kahneman, D. (2012). *Thinking, Fast and Slow.* London, UK: Penguin Group.

[2] Begley, E. (2024). Does sacking a manager help you avoid relegation? *BBC Sport,* online. Available at: https://www.bbc.co.uk/sport/football/articles/c0kv7ym5k2vo. Accessed March 2025.

[3] Smith, A. (2020). Does sacking a Premier League manager improve results? *Sky Sports,* online. Available at https://www.skysports.com/football/news/11096/11128604/does-sacking-a-premier-league-manager-improve-results. Accessed March 2025.

[4] Ouyang, L. Wu, J., Jiang, X. et al. (2022). Training language models to follow instructions with human feedback. *Cornell University.* https://cdn.openai.com/papers/Training_language_models_to_follow_instructions_with_human_feedback.pdf.

[5] Agrawal, A., Gans, J. et al. (2023). How large language models reflect human judgment. Harvard Business Review. https://hbr.org/2023/06/how-large-language-models-reflect-human-judgment.

Chapter 4 – Predictions & Pundits

[1] Kahneman, D. (2012). *Thinking, Fast and Slow.* London, UK: Penguin Group.

[2] Gladwell, M. (2009). *Outliers.* New York, NY: Back Bay Books.

Chapter 5 – Form & The Zone

[1] Chhabra, B., & Szabo, A. (2024). Placebo and nocebo effects on sports and exercise performance: a systematic review update. *Nutrients, 16*(13). https://doi.org/10.3390/nu16131975.

[2] Stamatelopoulou, F., Pezirkianidis, C. et al (2018). "Being in the zone": a systematic review on the relationship of psychological correlates and the occurrence of flow experiences in sports' performance. *Psychology, 9*(8), 2011-2030. https://doi.org/10.4236/psych.2018.98115.

[3] Waikar, S. (2023). Getting into "The Zone" isn't about perfection, it's about uncertainty. *Insights by Stanford Business,* online. Available at https://www.gsb.stanford.edu/insights/getting-zone-isnt-about-perfection-its-about-uncertainty. Accessed January 2025.

[4] Lochbaum, M., Stoner, E. et al. (2022). Sport psychology and performance meta-analyses: a systematic review of the literature. *Public Library of Science, 17*(2). https://doi.org/10.1371/journal.pone.0263408.

Chapter 6 – Referee & Umpire Bias

[1] McCarrick, D., Bilalic, M. et al. (2021). Home advantage during the COVID-19 pandemic: analyses of European football leagues. *Psychology of Sport and Exercise, 56*(9). https://doi.org/10.1016/j.psychsport.2021.102013.

[2] Dohmen, T. (2008). The influence of social forces: evidence from the behavior of football referees. *Economic Inquiry, 46*(3), 411-424. https://doi.org/10.1111/j.1465-7295.2007.00112.x.

[3] Erikstad, M., & Johansen, B. (2020). Referee bias in professional football: favoritism toward successful teams in potential penalty situations. *Frontiers in Sports and Active Living*. https://doi.org/10.3389/fspor.2020.00019.

[4] Dawson, P., Dobson, S. et al (2007). Are football referees really biased and inconsistent?: evidence on the incidence of disciplinary sanction in the English Premier League. *Journal of the Royal Statistical Society, 170*(1), 231-250. https://www.jstor.org/stable/4623144.

[5] Jones, M., Paull, G. et al (2010). The impact of a team's aggressive reputation on the decisions of association football referees. *Journal of Sports Sciences, 20*(12), 991-1000. https://doi.org/10.1080/026404102321011751.

[6] Krenn, B. (2013). The impact of uniform colour on judging tackles in Association football. *Psychology of Sport & Exercise, 15*(2), 222-225. https://doi.org/10.1016/j.psychsport.2013.11.007.

[7] Van Quaquebeke, N., & Glessner, S. (2010). How embodied cognitions affect judgments: height-related attribution bias in football foul calls. *Journal of Sport and Exercise, 32*(1), 3-22. https://doi.org/10.1123/jsep.32.1.3.

[8] Pope, B., & Pope, N. (2015). Own-nationality bias: evidence from UEFA Champions League football referees. *Economic Inquiry, 53*(2), 1292-1304. https://doi.org/10.1111/ecin.12180.

[9] Sasheti, A., Gregory-Smith, I. et al. (2015). Home bias in officiating: evidence from international cricket. *Journal of the Royal Statistical Society, 178*(3), 741-755. https://doi.org/10.1111/rssa.12086.

[10] Shivakumar, R. (2015). What technology says about decision-making: evidence from cricket's Decision Review System (DRS). http://dx.doi.org/10.2139/ssrn.2700405.

Chapter 7 – Winning & Losing

[1] Pope, D., & Schweitzer, M. (2011). Is Tiger Woods loss averse? Persistent bias in the face of experience, competition, and high stakes. *American Economic Review, 101*(1), 129-157. https://doi.org/10.1257/aer.101.1.129.

[2] Schneemann, S., & Deutscher, C. (2016). Intermediate information, loss aversion, and effort: empirical evidence. *Economic Inquiry, 55*(4), 1759-1770. https://doi.org/10.1111/ecin.12420.

[3] Yang, Q., & Zhao, Y. (2023). Risk-taking, loss aversion, and performance feedback in dynamic and heterogeneous tournaments. *Frontiers in Psychology, 9*(14). https://doi.org/10.3389/fpsyg.2023.1223369.

[4] Babatunde, B., & Rob, S. (2008). Do sports fans really value uncertainty of outcome? Evidence from the English Premier League. *International Journal of Sport Finance, 3*(3), 146-155.

[5] Humphreys, B., & Pérez, L. (2019). Loss aversion, upset preference, and sports television viewing audience size. *Journal of Behavioral and Economics, 78*(2), 61-67. https://doi.org/10.1016/j.socec.2018.12.002.

Chapter 8 – Crowds & Fandom

[1] Sinclair, A. The dark side of human behaviour: the impact of the Zimbardo deindividuation study. Available at https://achology.com/psychology/the-dark-side-of-human-behavior-the-impact-of-the-zimbardo-deindividuation-study/. Accessed March 2025.

[2] Le Bon, G. (1977). *The Crowd: A Study of the Popular Mind.* New York: Penguin Books.

[3] Johnson, R., & Downing, L. (1979). Deindividuation and valence of cues: Effects on prosocial and antisocial behaviour. *Journal of Personality and Social Psychology, 37*(9), 1532-1538. https://doi.org/10.1037/0022-3514.37.9.1532.

[4] Wann, D. (2024). The psychology of sports fans. *Speaking of Psychology.* Available at https://www.apa.org/news/podcasts/speaking-of-psychology/sports-fans. Accessed March 2025.

[5] Dolton, P., & MacKerron, G. (2018). Is football a matter of life and death – or is it more important than that? *National Institute of Economic and Social Research.* Available at https://niesr.ac.uk/publications/football-matter-life-and-death-or-it-more-important?type=discussion-papers. Accessed March 2025.

[6] Eyal, Nir.(2021). How do sports teams develop such loyal fans? *Psychology Today.* Available at https://www.psychologytoday.com/gb/blog/automatic-you/202107/how-do-sports-teams-develop-such-loyal-fans. Accessed March 2025.

ABOUT THE AUTHOR

Robert was a professional Economist for more than 20 years, working in London and Singapore. Returning to the UK in 2014, he completed several psychology courses, including a Certificate of Higher Education. He also obtained a Diploma in Cognitive Behavioural Therapy. He has Bachelor's and Master's degrees in Economics from the University of Warwick.

Robert is the author of several successful self-help and applied psychology books including "Fallibilities & Peculiarities," "Better Mental Health in Ten Words," "The Constructive Solution" and "The Power of Comparison."

As well as writing, Robert works as a voluntary reading helper at a local primary school in Kent.

Printed in Dunstable, United Kingdom

64805813R00087